T0067121

First Edition

TEACHING ETIQUETTES
FOR A SUCCESSFUL TEACHER

Essential Book For A Successful Teacher

Manaf Ibrahim Katonga

authorHOUSE®

AuthorHouse™ UK
1663 Liberty Drive
Bloomington, IN 47403 USA
www.authorhouse.co.uk
Phone: 0800.197.4150

Author Credits Editor: K. Kasambara

Published by AuthorHouse   02/05/2015

ISBN: 978-1-4969-9071-6 (sc)
ISBN: 978-1-4969-9072-3 (e)

Contents

Preface

It is of outstanding time to thank Almighty Lord who has made it possible to complete writing this book. This book is a unique book in education which can be used, but not limited to, by teachers in both government and private schools. The benefits of the book goes beyond the class teacher, as other beneficiaries can be head teachers, school committee members, parents, governments and other school stakeholders.

It was in my best interest to write a book regarding education as I have been a teacher for over 10 years, and found that there are a number of areas that a lot of teachers forget to understand in the teaching career. This book gives the teacher a number of areas that he/she can concentrate on, to make his/her job easy.

I, therefore, encourage teachers, parents, school committee members, governments to buy the book so that they help education in schools. The book concludes that, if the education system is to work well, it requires joint efforts of all stakeholders.

ACKNOWLEDGEMENT

My acknowledgment goes to the following people:

- ➢ My mum and dad for the tireless effort to nurse and educate me.
- ➢ My wife, Sarah for her continuous love and support to write this book.
- ➢ My children: Siyat, Munirah, Munawwarah and Ibrahim for their patience and love.
- ➢ Mr Kasambara for editing the book
- ➢ All people who helped in all means but don't want to be mentioned.

INTRODUCTION

Teaching is a process where a teacher imparts knowledge to the students by using various methods. Teaching has been a practice for many years, since the creation of the universe. As the time and environment evolve so are the changes about teachers, students, methods of teaching, contents of education and places where teaching takes place. Teaching has been an integral part of the successful societies. Unfortunately, power and politics were used to marginalize certain societies from getting viable education by discriminating them on the basis of color, race, religion, region, gender and others. The lack of balanced disseminating of relevant education to masses has resulted to failed societies and nations.

In the teaching process, there are vital components that make education successful. If these three components are presented before you: a book, a teacher and a school, what will you choose having known that all these are very important in education? A wise person will choose a teacher. The teacher has been the main player in the education system. In the old age where there were no buildings of schools, no books, the teacher was the only available source of education. When people ask the elderly people in other countries about their education, they will answer that they got education without books and well structured buildings that were used as schools. Teachers were the only available resource of education. Whenever they wanted to write something they used to write it on sand or on their hands. It was a common phrase that "they got their education under the tree". Even though such situations are not commonly experienced in the developed world, the situation is apparent in most developing and under- developed countries. Children still learn in difficult situations such as lack of proper infrastructure, lack of books, lack of well trained teachers, and others.

A teacher is able to teach students at any given circumstances. A teacher has a vital role to play for the spread of knowledge to the people. He is able to transfer his knowledge to people without books and classrooms. Some people can argue that it is possible to get education without the teacher. They can read the books and attain knowledge without having interaction with the teacher, or they can use internet to source variable information. What we should know is that there are "visible teachers" and "invisible teachers". Visible teachers are those teachers who teach people directly while invisible teachers are those who give people knowledge without any contact with them. Invisible teachers are people who write books, design and upload information to the web pages by the use of the Internet. People who write books and provide information in the internet can be regarded as invisible teachers. Without such people who write books and put information in the websites, no one will be able to get relevant information from the books and the Internet.

A shortage of teachers in many places is one of the major problems in the education systems in many countries. Governments face challenges because of inadequate number of teachers in schools, colleges and universities. The number of teachers is diminishing year by year in most countries. This lack of teachers has caused governments and other stakeholders like religious groups, NGO to bring in "fly-by-night" or inexperienced teachers. As a result education of the children is being affected.

In the past, when learners were asked what they wanted to be when they grew older, many of them chose to be teachers. But when the same question is asked to the students of today, few of them choose teaching as a career. It appears that teaching is no longer considered to be an admirable job to many people because of many negative factors that is driving people away from the teaching sector. Some of the restraining forces from teaching are the lack of respect that teachers face from learners, insufficient salaries, development of new careers and the change of psychological contract of many people.

Teachers in the past enjoyed their career, not because they were earning good salaries, but the environment they lived made them love teaching and were dedicated to the teaching career. Students and communities listened and respected them. In today's world, things are different; there is high level of disrespect, fighting teachers. In some of the developed countries there are incidences where pupils shoot and kill teachers. The school environment is increasingly becoming unbearable. Violence in school is high. In some developed countries students even bring guns, knives and dangerous weapons to school. The teachers are no longer in control of classes, but the students are. Teachers do not have powers they used to have before because of the behavior of students and type of government laws where teachers have little control over the behavior and attitudes of the students.

Some people refrain from joining the teaching sector because of the amount of money that teachers receive is very little in most countries. The teaching professional is one of the low paid jobs compared to other types of jobs in various countries. Governments being the major employers of teachers in the world do not give sufficient amount of salary to teachers as they were supposed to get. While many refrain from teaching job, many teachers are quitting and joining other careers which they believe will provide good salaries and honor. The burning question is "If everyone is running away from teaching career then who is going to teach our children in schools, colleges and universities or any other higher learning institution? If there is lack of teachers in learning institutions what type of future are we building for our children?

It is time for people to realize that teaching is a very important job for the successful nation. The governments should bring measures to motivate people to take teaching career very seriously. There should be good improvement in the teaching environment, as well as in teachers' salary scales. There should be an increase of teacher-training centers. Teaching is a skill that not everyone can have. Not every person who learnt accounting will be able to teach accounting subjects to other people. It requires certain behavior, skill and training. A person can have enough knowledge but because he does not know how to teach he will fail to transfer his knowledge to the students. For education to be viable there must be a good chain of communication among the teachers, students, parents and the governments, or other interested stakeholders. The book starts with a section of the teacher, followed by teaching aids and then the role of parents and finally it concludes by looking into school management.

Qualities Of A Good Teacher

Teachers require specific skills when disseminating knowledge to different levels of education and the age group of students he/she teaches. The age group of students can be divided into six: pre-school, early primary school, mid primary school, late primary school, high school, college / university. Teachers who will be responsible for different level of students will need specific skills that are needed for that particular level. For example, skills that are needed for preschool level of children will be different to college/university level. In preschool, learners are very young, they like playing and eating regularly, and also those who are very young, like to sleep in between before going home. The teacher of this level requires skills that are: more entertaining, guarding, directing. In college/university, learners are adults, career oriented, focused. Teacher/lecturer at college/university level needs to posses skills such as mentorship, coaching, counseling.

There are certain qualities that a good teacher need to possess, some of them are: knowledge, patience, psychology, cleanliness, punctuality, self control, good health, fitness, good voice, communicable body language.

KNOWLEDGE

Subject knowledge is type of the knowledge that a teacher of such particular subject must have. The teacher must have enough knowledge of the subject so that he/she will be able to teach his learners with confidence and learners will also have confidence on the teacher which will motivate them to enjoy the subject. When the teacher does not have sufficient knowledge of the subject he teaches at school expanding his knowledge is very important. The insufficient knowledge of the teacher can come from three main areas: the changing of subjects and contents because of changing of time; teaching of subjects that the teacher is not expert on; teaching of subjects that the teacher did not study.

Type of subjects, contents of subjects and students that were taught 50 years ago are different to present time. In the past, teachers had few learners in class and the methods that were used enabled them to teach few students. The number of subjects and their contents were small comparing to present situations. But today many institutions have a lot of students. Subjects and contents of subjects that are not relevant to present century have been changed and replaced with relevant information.

The changing of subjects, contents and type of students have been influenced by the advancement of technology, globalization, changing of societies and politics. Technology has improved a lot of things in the education sector. Printing of books, production of written materials, and introduction of many devices has made it easy for the teachers to teach well. The absence of technology in the past made it difficult for the teacher to execute his/her knowledge properly.

Adapting to the changes of teaching environment and technology in particular, the teacher teaching in the past where there was no technology might face numerous challenges. Challenges will include learning new things so that he/she will be able to teach learners properly in today's world. He/she needs to be a computer literate and have knowledge of printing machines and other devices. Without such knowledge he/she will have a problem of transferring his knowledge to his/her students because this generation is advancing with technology. There so many ways of how such kind of teachers can increase their knowledge to meet the current requirements. He/she can enroll in colleges/universities to study relevant courses; reading relevant books; attending workshops/seminars, use of internet and technologies.

Imagine a teacher who comes into a class but does not know what to teach! He will stand there and talk stories but will fail to educate the learners. When the students ask him questions he will not be able to answer properly. It will be embarrassing to tell the students that he does not know to answer the question. This type of answer will not give students confidence about the teacher.

The knowledge that is required will also involve knowing how to deal with the changing behavior of students. The behavior of the students has changed. Technology and politics are the main factors that influence the behavior of students in many societies and nations. Other Students chat with friends in social media while in class. There is growing lack of concentration among many students when they are in class. In addition the number of laws many government implement are giving power to students and limiting power of teachers. Teachers are therefore required to attend training in order to understand the laws and also to know how to deal with new trends of behavior among the students.

Knowledge of the social issues of the society is very important for the teacher. In the past most teachers were coming from the societies they taught. They knew culture and belief of their students. But today, there is a migration and movement of people from one place to the other which expose them to different beliefs and culture. Teachers are also in the move and are exposed to different beliefs and culture. Therefore they need to have knowledge of the new beliefs and culture because failing to do so teachers may offend students unknowingly of their belief and culture which can result to poor communication between teachers and the students.

PATIENCE

Patience is an important tool for a successful teacher. Many teachers are short-tempered, and some of them want immediate results from the students. They feel angry very quickly when a student does something wrong and as a result they respond by either stopping a lesson in class or hitting the student. Teachers need to control themselves from anger so that they can solve the problem without causing any harm. Hitting the student while angry might cause a serious harm, for example breaking hands or legs of the student.

Teaching is a process which requires a great deal of patience from the teacher. Not all students in the class have similar levels of understanding. Some are quick in learning while others take time to understand the same thing. If the teacher is not patient with the slow learners, he will not be able to teach them. When slow learners see that the teacher is not interested in them because they are slow learners, they may leave the school or they may become mischievous or plan to possibly harm the teacher. Anger management is important to every teacher and every human being. Teachers should know that they are teaching children coming from different backgrounds. It will be difficult for all of them to behave the same.

The teacher is like a parent of the child. Children do not behave the same although they may come from the same mother and father. One child may be slower than the other. When the teacher exercises patience with his learners he/she will be happy when he will see the results of his/her effort. There are circumstances where a student was a slow learner or a naughty child, but the teacher's patience helped him to be a successful person. Students like them remember the past and acknowledge how the teacher helped them. Not all naughty pupils will end up being naughty and not all good pupils will end up being good students when they grow up. Students can change to either direction when they are growing.

Patience is a psychological part of a human being. It is the capacity to accept or tolerate delay, trouble, or suffering without getting angry or upset or/ and it is the state of endurance under difficult circumstances, which can mean persevering in the face. It is when a person positively accepts the challenges he/she is currently facing while finding ways to solve them. Challenges can either come from internal system of the person such as diseases or from external environment such as provocation from people, redundancy from work, bankruptcy, etc. A person may exercise patience after a certain problem and fails to exercise patience for the other problem. It depends on how big the problem is. Good examples of patience may include a person who is sick and taking medicine but not negatively thinking about his disease, or person who is bankrupt but remain strong instead of winging and trying to commit suicide. Good examples of impatience is when a person facing a problem fails to control himself/herself and negatively find solutions that will negatively harm him/her such suicide. The end result of impatience is that people lose life, bad reputation, and divorce, lose work, drop schooling, and lose friends.

Anger is found to be a disease that destroys patience easily. It is well known that when a person is angry the level of thinking drops. The more a person becomes angry the more his/her thinking capacity drops. It is believed that a certain drop of thinking capacity because anger can be equal to a certain drop of thinking capacity that is caused by drinking of alcohol or other intoxicants like drugs. There is behavioral correlation between an angry person and a drunken person in some other people. Shouting, fighting, and swearing, just to mention a few, are some of the behaviors that are found on both angry and a drunken person. In many circumstances both the angry and a drunken person blame themselves on the action they took after they became angry or drunken.

SELF-CONTROL

The teacher as a human being experiences emotional issues and sometimes loss control. When the teacher has problems and fails to control himself will not be able to teach the learners properly. He/she will not have the energy to prepare the lesson. He/she must put into consideration that in some countries, there are teachers who are teaching while the bombs fall nearby, guns fired on a daily basis, they don't eat good food but their performance in class is not affected.

Self control is the ability to control one's emotions, behavior, and desires to gain reward or to avoid a problem. Examples of emotions are: fear, anger, sadness, depression, stress, joy, disgust, etc. Some of the factors that cause negative emotions such as stress, depression, sadness and anger include business bankruptcy, marriage problems, work retrenchment, challenging school work. Negative emotions; tend to spiral out of control, especially immediately after they have been triggered. In time, these sorts of emotions can grow like weeds, slowly conditioning the mind to function on detrimental feelings and dominating daily life. So how can we avoid operating on the wrong types of feelings and master our emotions under the harshest of circumstances? Do not react right away. Reacting immediately to emotional triggers can be an immense mistake. Before refuting the trigger with emotional argument, take a deep breath and stabilize the overwhelming impulse. Whenever you are confronted with an emotion which is making you feel or think something bad, force it out of your mind and replace it with different thought. The other way to reduce negative emotions is to forgive your emotion triggers who may be your family members, yourself, your friends, your students, etc.

Self control from desirers is also important for a human being. People have different desires to fulfill their needs. Below is a pyramid showing Maslow's needs hierarchy.

Maslow's theory is based on the following: people continuously want things. People always want more, and what they want depends on what they already have. As soon as one need is satisfied, another takes its place. People can therefore never be fully satisfied, and they behave in a particular way to satisfy a need or a combination of needs. The desires can be according to Maslow's theory of needs: physiological, safety, social, ego and self actualization. The desires can be attained individually or a combine of desires depending on the ability to achieve such desires. The ability to achieve desires will depend of the kind of the desire. Other desires will require physical strength of the person, others desires will depend on the financial ability of the person, and other desires will depend on the external forces of a human being like, peer pressure, good marketing, income changes, globalization, emigration, media, etc.

The Ability/Desire figure below illustrates three situations where Ability is measured with desire: The situations are labeled A, B and C.

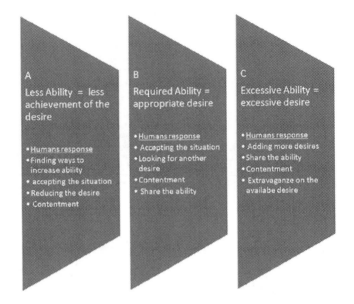

Situation A: Less Ability = Less achievement of the desire

People sometimes fulfill only a certain part of their desires because of the level of ability the people possess. According to the diagram above, people may respond to the situation of less ability= less achievement by using four options: Finding ways to increase ability, accepting the situation, reducing the desire and have contentment. Finding ways to increase ability can be either positive or negative. This way of response may sometimes be a tempting one. For example, if the person desires to have a mansion or good business but does not have enough money to do so, he/she may think of unnecessary measures like theft, corruption, fraud, robbery,etc in order to fulfill his/her desires. The remaining ways of response in this situation is very positive; they help the person to have self control.

Situation B: Required Ability= Appropriate desire

This situation entails that the person is able to fulfill his/her desires because he/she has required amount of ability. It is in this situation that people tend to look for another desire once the other one is achieved corresponding to Maslow's theory of needs. When a person looks for another desire will require addition ability to fulfill it. The person may return to situation A. The other responses of this situation can be accepting the situation; contentment and sharing the ability will help the person to have self control.

Situation C: Excessive Ability = Excessive desire

This situation entails that the person has excessive ability to achieve the preferred desires. Because of the excessive ability the person add more tremendous desires and fulfill them excessively. For example, the person wants to eat food; he has excessive ability/money. He buys food beyond his desires and eats excessively which results into stomach discomfort. Any excessive expenditure of ability is regarded as extravagance and always carries problems. To exercise self control in situation C a person should have contentment and share ability to other people.

More examples of desires, ability and contentment

Example 1: Some rich people fail to sleep well even if they have good bed and good foods while some people who sleep in the streets sleep without blankets, beds and food have deep sleep.

Example 2: When you visit rural area will find people living in grass roofed small houses without running water and electricity but appear happy and enjoy life. But when you visit rich people, in their mansions, expensive cars parked in their garages, maid-servants around them and surplus money in the bank experience unhappy life and end up committing suicide.

PSYCHOLOGY

The teacher requires fundamental understanding of the psychology knowledge for him/her to be able to understand students is teaching. With the psychological knowledge the teacher is able to monitor every student's personality system. Students' behavior may comprise introverted, naughty, stubborn, violent, etc. Such behaviors of the students may come up because of the environment surrounding them. It is common nowadays to find students coming from bad homes where there is regular fighting between mother and father, where there is great abusive of children. Such type of environment will influence certain behavior of students at school.

Learner's behavior can change. There are circumstances where the learner can be a well performing student in class but all of sudden he/she might drop to lower standard. When the teacher experiences a change of behavior of a particular student, he/she must find reasons why the learner is behaving in such way. It will require good skills to find a root cause of the problem. Other learners are very confidential and timid. Some ways that can help the teacher to unpack problems from such kind of students may include; having a secret meeting with the student and promise him/her that you will not reveal the problem to other people; interviewing parents, family members, and friends. When problems are unpacked teacher heeds to help the student overcome the problem. Other problems like rape are very serious that will require involvement of the people with authority. Counseling and other forms of support to the student will be needed to help the student. The teacher must always be alert of the behavioral patterns of his/her students.

Psychology is concerned mainly with the study of human behavior, with traits of the individual and membership of small social groups. The main focus of attention is on the individual as a whole person, or what can term the "personality systems", including, for example, perceptions, attitudes and motives. Personality systems can be influenced by social, political, economical and cultural background such as religion, language, morals, food and beliefs. For example, people in India have different languages and forms of food comparing to people living in Malawi. People behave very differently.

Although a group of people can have similarities in certain behaviors but individuals are different in their thinking and perceptions. It is possible that a person coming from the same location belonging to the same religion but behaves differently. The difference of behavior can change for example, because of poverty or richness. Behavior that surrounds poverty may include lack of confidence, fear, praising the rich. Behavior that surrounds some rich people may include pride, confidence and self esteem. Children grew up differently one with parents and the other as an orphan, will also have different behavior.

Using the Katonga Behaviour Change Model teachers will successfully deal with the changing behavior of the students. The Katonga Behaviour change model has five steps as illustrated below:

The example of a sudden change of performance on a girl child is used.

Katonga Behaviour Change Model

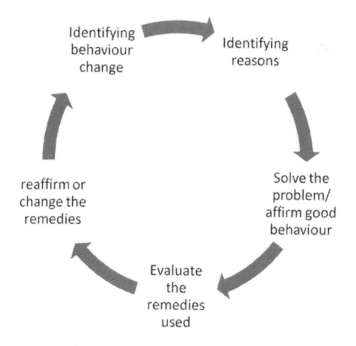

Identifying behaviour change

Identifying reasons

reaffirm or change the remedies

Solve the problem/ affirm good behaviour

Evaluate the remedies used

Step one: Identifying behavior change: In this step the teacher compares the behavior of the student with his/her previous behavior. The teacher is able to identify certain changes of student's behavior. Using the example above, the teacher finds out that the girl student who was performing well is class has dramatically dropped in areas of exams, tests, class participation and has lost confidence.

Step two: Identifying reasons for change: In this step the teacher finds ways to talk to the student, either in the office privately or other places deemed fit for the student. It is a difficult step that is used to find a root cause of the problem. It requires good communication skills from the teacher. Measures of persuasion, encouragement and motivation are very important during this step. If the teacher fails to find the problem, then he/she must involve other interested people such as friends of the student, parents, headmaster/principal of the school, etc. In our example the teacher took the girl to teacher's home and instructed his wife to question the girl. The girl was open to tell the teacher's wife about issues that were happening to her. The identified reasons were that her father lost the job; therefore they sometimes slept without food in their house.

Step three: Solve the problem/ affirm good behavior: In this step the teacher can suggest certain solutions/ remedies to help solving the problem. In our example, the teacher took the matter to the principal who then introduced feeding scheme at the school. If the change of behavior is towards good, the teacher can also identify the reasons. During identification of the reasons the teacher can complement the student and encourage him/her to continue with the good behavior.

<u>Step four: evaluate the remedies used:</u> In this step the teacher after a certain period should evaluate solutions used to solve the problem to know if they are working. Using our example above, the teacher finds that the student is able to perform well again.

<u>Step five: reaffirm/ change the remedies:</u> In this step, if the remedies/solutions are found to be working, then continuation with such particular solutions is very important. In our example, school feeding continued and the principal introduced different types of food in the school feeding scheme. If the remedies/ solutions tend to be failing, new solutions can me suggested. In our example helping the student's father can be alternative solution to the problem.

CLEANLINESS

Cleanliness of a person is regarded as removing dirty of the body, clothes and place primarily by the use of water. Taking care of the body has many forms but the most important and essential is the bath a person takes by the use of water. Different people have different ways of bathing, but the principal remain the same for many people where water is used to clean the body from the head to the toe. Although some people take days to bath but it is advisable to bath every day. Water reenergizes the body. Similarly washing clothes is important for the person. The economic position of the person determines how he/she wants his/her clothes to be washed. Others use soap and other chemicals while others only use water. The primary washing of clothes is when the bad smell is removed from the clothes. The place where the person sit, sleep or use it for other ways should be cleaned regularly. Sweeping, dusting and the use of water helps to keep the place clean. For the teacher, other things that he/she uses like books, pens, pencils should remain clean.

IMPORTANT THINGS FOR THE TEACHER TO CLEAN

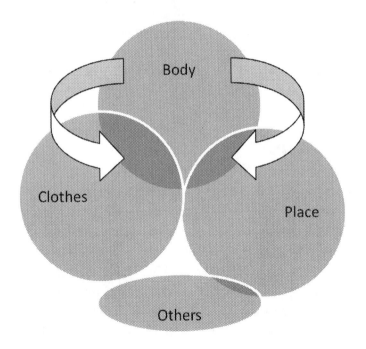

The main purpose of cleanliness for the person is to look nice and prevent him/her from diseases that can arise because of dirtiness. If the teacher lacks cleanliness in his life, he may get sick from dangerous germs. It is not impressive to see a person coming from a very beautiful house but his body is always dirty and badly smelling. Or to see the teacher who bathes well and clean clothes but his/her place of working or sleeping is very dirty. There should be a good link of cleanliness of the person from the body, place, clothes and other things he/she uses in his life. It is the responsibility of every teacher to clean his/her body.

Some other people have "modernized bathing". They use only perfumes and disregard water. Instead of bathing, they wake up in the morning, brush their teeth, comb their hair and apply perfume on their bodies and clothes, off they go to work. As long as they smell nicely they do not regard bathing as most important. There are possibilities that people may get sick when they only apply perfumes onto their bodies and ignoring bathing.

Neatness goes hand in hand with cleanliness. Therefore teachers should take neatness as part of their daily school life. Clothes change person's image. A person may look charming and presentable while other may look differently. Even if the teacher may have very few clothes but as long as he keeps them clean and look neat it gives good image to the students. Neatness can be a source of respect from the students to their teachers. The students feel impressed when see that their teachers dress well. The teachers being the mirror of the students, neatness of the teachers can encourage the students to maintain cleanliness and neatness as the teachers do. People believe that action speaks louder than words. How will teachers give a lesson of cleanliness while they fail to be clean?

For the teachers to avoid embarrassment by the students should be well-groomed. For example, the teacher enters a classroom with untidy hair and smelling badly, what will be the reaction of the learners? Students may start mocking the teacher and even laughing at him/her. The teacher will then become angry and beat the children laughing at him/her which may result into stopping the lesson.

PUNCTUALITY

Life revolves around time. People are born grow and die within time. Duration of birth, growth is different from human beings to other creations. Life span during growth of a human being is commonly within on century. By using time people calculate hours, days, months, years and use for different purposes. People are able to evaluate the benefits gained within a particular time. For example, people evaluate performance of an organization after one year or so; teachers evaluate number of lessons covered for a particular term. Without the use of time people will not be able to know the year, the school term, the financial year, etc.

LIFE ARROW FOR THIS WORLD

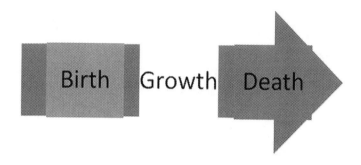

The good teacher is the one who uses time effectively "time management". The teacher that uses time effectively covers syllabus. For the teacher to achieve benefits of time teaching schools, colleges or universities should be punctual for his/ her duty.

Some other teachers are reluctant during the first and second quarter of term. They come late to work, and increase absenteeism. When they see that the term is close to finish is when they show enthusiasm teaching the students. Because the teacher is late to cover the syllabus, he/she rushes to teach the lesson which affects the quality and performance of education rendered. There are a number of effects that students suffer from the poor attendance of the teacher. The effects may include stress, anger and poor relationship with the teacher. Students may change subjects and/ or careers they pursue because of poor attendance of the teacher.

Teachers coming late to school should know that they oppress learners. The work which was supposed to be finished within two days may take longer because of the lost time. If the teacher is under pressure because of the time wasted, he/she will then teach children without following the correct procedures. Non-punctual teachers tend to be absentee teachers. They stay away at home without any specific reason.

COUNSELLING AND ADVICE

Teachers should have skills of counseling students. Students face problems that may seem small to big people but to them are very big. Using counseling skills will help the student to solve the problems is facing amicably.

Children nowadays face tremendous challenges that require counseling. Children face challenges like rape, abusive family, neglecting parents, and other abuses. In class there will be students who will need counseling. Many learners dropped school, committed suicide because of lack of counseling. Children take their lives because they fail in their examinations, or losing something. Some other reasons could be avoided when counseling is used. A teacher should narrate stories of hope and achievement of people like Nelson Mandela, Malcom X, Bill Gate and others. Read stories to them of people who suffered but later on succeeded in life. If the problems are big the teachers can use counseling organizations to help the students.

The fall of family and community institutions has caused the establishment of counseling organizations in many areas such marriage counseling organizations, children counseling organizations, financial counseling organizations, school counseling organizations, etc. Many people live under very stressful life because of unachieved expectations, bank credits, business bankruptcy, divorce, death of a family member, etc. They counseling so that their children should not be affected.

Family institution of the past encouraged the value of orphans. In the past orphans were less heard of. If the family member died and left behind children, the remaining family members sat down to see how they would help the children and a custodian was chosen. He/she was able to look after the children without showing favor to his own children. Other children grew up without even knowing that they were orphans. If there was something wrong in the family the elderly people had a duty to solve the problem without favoritism. Children were less stressed and concentrated on school.

Many orphans whom we see in the streets today have uncles, aunties, cousins or relatives who are wealthy but do not want to take care of them. Nowadays, a brother does not like a brother, a sister, uncle or any family member. Nowadays children are taught that relatives are only people born from the same mother and father. They are not taught about the extended family. People need to give good advice to their children so that they grow up with good morals and behavior.

The helping circle below can help people when prioritizing assistance. The circle illustrates that the best way of helping is to start with your family and parents then grandparents and aunties followed by the cousins and finally any other person. It is not good to ignore helping your cousins when are suffering and helping any other person. If people use the circle below will reduce stress in the families like the stress that children of family members experience that is resulted, for example, from lack of fees, insufficient, etc.

Helping Circle

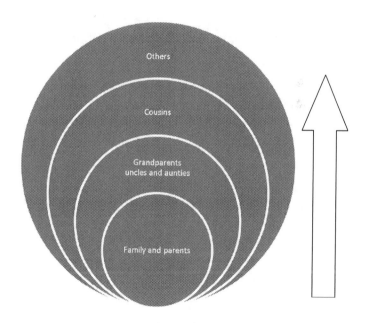

HEALTH AND FITNESS

Understanding the diseases and measures to curb such diseases will help teachers to be healthy so that they will be able to carry out their duties properly. How are they going to prepare their work when they are sick? How are they going to walk in the classrooms when they fail to walk? The teacher should lead a healthy lifestyle to keep his body in good shape. The healthy teacher is an admirable teacher. He is the anchor of the community. There are many ways how the teacher can exercise. It is good to refer to health professionals or doctors who will explain what kind of exercises and foods that are good for the teacher.

Diseases affect performance of a person and impinge the development of organizations and the nations. The number of diseases that people face is countless and the list is continuous. People suffer from simple diseases to complicated diseases. Diseases like flue, headache, asthma, high blood pressure, cancer, HIV and AIDS are some of the diseases that affect people's performance at the workplace. There are times when the world witnessed presidents, ministers, managers quitting/ relinquishing their positions because of deteriorating of their health conditions. An organization that experiences a large number of sick employees fails to perform at an optimal standard.

A stable family is the one that has health people, a stable company is the one that has health workers and a health nation is a winning nation. Families, companies and nations have lost beloved people who died because of diseases. Every year governments increase health budgets to help the increased cases of diseases. Notably most large parts of health budgets are used to treat diseases and small amount is used for prevention of diseases. Families, organizations and governments that spend time and money to on prevention of diseases are successful. Many diseases that people suffer are because of ignoring prevention measures.

The main contributing factor to poor health is the type of food people eat. Failure to eat proper food at proper times is the major problem to many people. Some other people continuously eat junk foods. Junk foods are very much harmful to the body because if you continuously eat them cause diseases such as cancer, diabetes, increased blood pressure, heart disease. Other contributing factors are unprotected /un-prevented sex, pollutions, alcohol, drug abuse and lack of exercises.

The world requires people who are healthy and fit for them to be good presidents, ministers, managers because a healthy person is able to do work properly.

HIV & AIDS is a disease that has also caused many suffering and deaths of many skilled professionals, including teachers. Many people are suffering from this disease. The numbers of orphans are increasing almost every day because of HIV and AIDS. Many communities overlooked this pandemic and had a denial syndrome because of their strong religious and cultural values they promote. Because of self sufficient in their cocoon had impressions that will never be affected by HIV and AIDS and ignored to take measures to counter the pandemic. But today, such communities face the HIV and AIDS pandemic.

There are so many diseases that are associated to alcohol. Problems and diseases such as slurred speech, drossiness, vomiting, diarrhea, upset stomach, headaches, breathing difficulties, distorted vision, decreased perception and coordination, anemia, memory lapses, loss of productivity, increased family problems, broken relationship, high blood pressure, stroke, nerve damage, ulcers, etc. Alcohol is at rampant in many countries. There is an increase consumption of alcohol mainly by the youths and women. The increase is correlated to the increase of cases of diseases that come because of alcohol.

Cigarette smoking is the most preventable causes of illness and death. Smoking harms nearly every organ of the body. Smoking causes many diseases and reduces the health of smokers in general. Cigarette smoking causes reduced circulation by narrowing the blood vessels and puts smokers at risk of developing peripheral vascular diseases. Smoking causes heart attack, stroke, lung cancers, asthma, emphysema, ulcers, miscarriage, difficult to get pregnant, etc.

MEASURES TO REMAIN HEALTH AND FIT

There are various measures to curb the diseases such as prevention, eating healthy foods, abstaining from adultery and remain faithful to your spouse, exercising and fasting.

EATING HEALTH FOODS

Eating a wide variety of foods (a balanced diet) from within and across each of the five food groups, in the amounts recommended. Eating many different foods helps maintain healthy, well – balanced and interesting diet that provides adequate nutrition. A healthy diet is the basis for a well- functioning body. It helps to maintain an ideal body weight, prevent diseases, and lead to better overall performance of the mind and body. Healthy eating includes fresh, whole foods, like fruits and vegetables, whole grains, low-fat dairy and lean protein. Eating healthy foods on a daily basis assist in helping to maintain the proper weight. Eating healthy to combat diseases like type 2 diabetes where obesity is a major risk factor in this disease. Other complications affiliated with type 2 diabetes are heart disease, blindness and kidney failure. A person should decrease the risk of type 2 diabetes by consuming food and beverages that are low in sugar. Eliminate food and drinks made with high-fructose. Substitute with herbal tea and water. These healthy alternatives help lower calories. Also eat salads, raw or steamed vegetables, and whole grains.

EXERCISING

If you don't use your body, you will surely lose it. Your muscle will become flabby and weak. Your heart and lungs won't function efficiently. And your joints will be stiff and easily injured. Inactivity is as much of health risk as smoking. Our bodies were meant to move—they actually crave exercise. Regular exercise is necessary for physical fitness and good health. It reduces the risk of heart disease, cancer, higher blood pressure, diabetes and other diseases. It can improve your appearance and delay the aging process. Exercise is a key to weight control because it burns calories. Once you begin to exercise regularly, you will discover many more reasons why exercise is so important to improving the quality of your life. Exercise reduces stress, lifts moods, and helps you sleep better. It can keep you looking and feeling younger throughout your entire life.

FASTING

Fasting helps to keep the person's body healthy. Some of the benefits of fasting are: Any intestinal microbes within the digestive tract are kept in check during fasting and are restricted from producing any poisons. During the fast people ought to become more active mentally and physically as well. Blood that is normally directed to the stomach after the meal is now diverted to other areas of the body, like the brain and other organs, hence the feelings of mental well-being and physical improvement. Sick or injured cells in the body are destroyed during fasting and subsequently replaced by new healthy cells. Fasting reduces the water quantities in the blood, skin and body thereby inducing the cure of any skin rash diseases. Individual with a high level of cholesterol can benefit by fasting which in turn lowers the cholesterol reading.

Voice and Body Language

In the classroom the teacher must know how to speak to his students. The teacher should make an assessment to determine students who have hearing problems. The student who has hearing problem should seat in front of the class and not at the back. The teacher should avoid screaming when teaching children or talking softly to such an extent that the children find it difficult to hear; he/she should use the level of voice in a balanced manner. He/she should talk to the students in a way that students will hear and understand him/her properly. Because there are words which when spoken fast mean something and when are spoken slowly will mean something else. For example words like "it and eat" sound the same but the difference is the use in the sentence and the speed of saying the word.

Being a teacher does not mean that you have to be serious at all times. If there is something to laugh about, laugh with the students in a good manner. There are times when a teacher has to joke with the learners in a respectable manner in order to gain their attention and good relationship. A teacher should know when to be strict and when to be soft to the students. The teacher should use simple words which are common to the children. Avoid using words that will make it difficult to understand the lesson. The other issues that the teacher should avoid are the use insulting words and vulgar language. Using insulting words to the learners will inevitably teach students such behavior. Use slang words are also not good when teaching students.

Speech is an influential tool of communication. It has managed to bring people together and sometimes brought about a lot of disharmony in the community to the extent of violence and deaths. Speech is used in schools, in business, and many other places. The type of voice, which comes from the mouth of a person, is different from person to person depending on physical capability and attitude. Some people don't know how to speak softly, they scream when they want to say something while other people do not know how to scream even if they are angry. The manner in which the voice of a person is used determines whether the person is respectful, arrogant, shy, hungry, in pain, happy, or sad. There are many factors that can cause people to change the way they speak, whether into respectful, arrogant and humbleness. Factors such as gaining wealthy, attaining good education, serving high positions may change the way people speak with other people. Humbleness is a good character for the human being, particularly for teachers.

Body language is also important in class environment. Effective teachers use body language to communicate with students, build rapport with them, and make them feel safe and supported. Face the student with arms uncrossed and relaxed, give them eye-to-eye contact, and pay attention to the students. The ability of a teacher to establish positive rapport with students is critical aspect of the teacher-learner relationship. The successful teacher blends both verbal and nonverbal communication skills in establishing good rapport with students and this has a direct correlation to student achievement. Test your understanding of your students and how your body language affects them by standing in the doorway of the room as your students shuffle in. This close contact sets up a naturally occurring single file line that calms them before they enter the classroom. If you look frazzled, you seem vulnerable; lack of confidence and is a red flag to students.

Poor posture –slumped shoulders, stomach sticking out-is not only physically unhealthy, but it can convey a whole range of attitudes. Avoid folding your arms, standing behind a desk, and using barriers. These behaviors block you off and make you appear unapproachable. Use the whole classroom. Walk around the students desks to show interest, and indicate approval with a head nod. Smile conveys happiness and encouragement. Frowns show sadness or anger. Big, open eye suggest fear or astonishment.

The way teachers' position in class should be at a place where students will be able to see them. They must be able to see all the students. Attention should be given to all of them not to specific students. If learners see that the teacher is not giving attention to all of them, others will sleep, or indulge in mischievous things without him/her knowing. When a teacher is using a writing board, white board or chalk board for example, should move towards the left and the right so that both sides of the students will be able to see what the teacher is writing on the board.

A Teacher Should Be Able To Use Syllabus And Prepare Lesson Plan

"Failing to prepare is preparing to fail" is a common connotation used by many people. It denotes the importance of planning. It is good to have things planned at every time. All aspects of life will require good planning to make things easy. For instance, if a man decides to go for a journey, but fails to arrange for his transport fee, the mode of transport, time for departure and arrival, will find it difficult to reach the desired destination.

Planning involves preparation, implementation and evaluation. Before doing anything preparation stage is very important. The preparation stage entails gathering all the necessary resources, analyzing how the desired goal will be achieved, analyzing and understanding the possible challenges that might infringe to achieve the desired goal. For example, before implementing the syllabus and the lesson plan, it is very important to see if there are essential resources that are needed to implement the syllabus in order to make it a successful plan. Resources that need to be considered so that the desired goal is achieved without many challenges are: availability of books, time allocation, and availability of teachers. It is awkward to find in many instances that the syllabus drawn by the education department or education councils is not achieved because of lack of resources. The problems should not be overlooked. If the planners fail to analyze the problems that may arise in the cause of the plan, the desired goal may not be achieved successfully. Lack of the resources may impact the education of students.

Implementation stage is a vital stage. It is the stage that determines the success of the desired goal. During this stage the syllabus or the lesson plan is implemented by using the resources organized in the preparation stage. During this stage is important to use necessary resources at the right time and at the right quantity. Most of the plans fail at the implementation stage mainly because of failing to allocate necessary resources at the right time and at the right quantity.

The final stage is the evaluation stage. It helps the teacher to compare the outcome with the plan that was set up. He/she will be able to find out if the outcome is the success or the failure. If the outcome is not good teachers should investigate reasons behind the failure so that they can be rectified.

Syllabus is a framework, plan and guideline of the work a teacher is going to teach. The syllabus is constructed from the whole years work according to the curriculum of the school. It helps the teacher to focus on the work given. From the syllabus, lesson plan is made which is every day lesson. It illustrates topic of the lesson, points to be covered, teaching aids to be used and the methods of teaching which will be used.

EXAMPLE OF SIMPLE LESSON PLAN

	Mountain view school **23 Citrus Drive** **Isipingo** **3002**

Grade/ Standard : 8
Subject: Economics
Teacher's name: Sumaya
Teacher's number : 44
Email :sumaya@gmail.com
Signature:

Date : 13/01/14	Day: Monday	Term: First

Topic/s : Business cycles

Points of concentration	• Recession, Trough, Boom, Pick, • Causes of business cycle • What government can do to avoid recession • Dangers of short term economic boom
Teaching Aids	Writing board, books and overhead projector
Methods of teaching	Explanation and questioning
Recommendations	The teacher has covered all prepared lesson. 80% of students understood the lesson.

37

Lesson plans is not a "railway" which cannot be changed easily. Lesson plan can be changed as long as it is focusing in achieving the syllabus and curriculum outlined. There are things that can cause changes to the lesson plan. For example, a teacher might get sick for a particular day therefore he/she can change the lesson plan of a particular date to another particular date. Strikes, death of student/teacher can be one of the contributing factors to changing of the lesson plan. A teacher should prepare his work a day or a week before going to class.

Consequences of failing to prepare lesson plans or plan well the lesson plans are many, some of them are: Aimless wandering, failure to achieve objectives, failing to source teaching materials or equipment. If the teacher doesn't plan lessons may fall into several traps; the teacher may wander aimlessly without achieving objectives of the course; what the teacher teaches may not lead to what he/she teaches later. Lack of planning can lead to poor or reduced learning time, frustration from both teachers and students.

A Teacher Should Be Able To Use Board And Chalk

Writing boards whether white or black plays a major role when teaching students. Some teachers neglect the use of the boards in the classroom; they prefer using books than the boards. Boards solve almost 50 percent of the work in class. For instance a teacher can teach while writing on the board, he/she use the board to write tests and use it when answering questions. He/she can draw and use different methods to explain something properly than using the book only. Children might not understand what the teacher is talking, but when the teacher writes the information on the board then the students are able to understand.

A teacher should use different color chalk/pen on the board to explain the lesson properly or to show the importance of the point. If the teacher does not have the colored chalk/pen, he/she can underline the important points, write in bold or use the capital letters where necessary. For example:

Subject	Example
Economics	a)When the country experiences economic boom, there is <u>high employment, economic growth,</u> etc. b)When the country experiences recession, there is decrease of <u>employment, economic activities drops,</u> etc.
English	a)**Yusuf** (ate) <u>banana</u> **SUBJECT** (Verb) <u>object</u>
Mathematics	a) 23+17 = **40** b) X + X = **2X** c) 90-70 = <u>20</u>

A teacher should use type of chalk that will make easy for the students to see what is written on the board. It is not good to use color chalk/pen that is similar to the color of the board. It makes it difficult for children to see what is written on the board. When the teacher is able to select good chalk/pen to use on the board, he/she should be mindful with the handwriting he/she uses on the board.

The handwriting / spelling should be good and write on straight lines. The teacher should not write small letters on the board, it makes difficult for the students seated at the back to see properly what is written on the board. If the spelling and handwriting of the teacher is not good on board will cause the students to write wrong things.

The teacher should also be careful when using the chalk/pen. It won't look nice when the teacher's clothes are messed by chalk dust. After completing the lesson, the teacher must dust himself and keep the chalk away from the reach of students. There are some children who steal chalk from the classroom and write rude things in the toilets and on the walls of the school classrooms.

A stick is commonly used in various schools to point things on the board. It helps the teacher to point important words or numbers on the board. Sometimes just talking without pointing the things confuses the students mostly the young ones. Therefore a good teacher will use a stick in class to explain points on the board. When the teacher is in front of the students and is using the board, he/she should move right and left. Doing so gives students in all directions to see what is written on the board. Failing to have good movement when using the board prevents other students from seeing what is written.

A Teacher Should Be Able To Speak Local Language

There are various local languages in the world, for example in Nigeria alone there are over 200 local languages and in South Africa there are 11 official languages. Language is used to communicate in different situations in human life. Language is used to spread peace in the world, is used in business, and is also used in education. Therefore the absence of language can prevent various activities of communication. Although languages are many, there are certain languages that are used in business world, for example, English, Arabic, Chinese, French, Portuguese, etc.

The teacher should be the person who knows the language of students. If English in a medium language but students or the society has a certain local language that is used, the teacher should be able also to know the local language. It vitalizes the sense of belonging to the society. If the teacher comes outside the community is teaching, knows different language, and should try to learn the language of his new community. Learning of the local language is a dual benefit to both the teacher and the students.

The benefits are:

○ The teacher is able to explain better the lessons to the students if they do not understand it better in official language used like English, Arabic, French, etc.

○ Students and the community feel happy as the teacher shows the sense of belonging to the community.

○ The teacher can understand when students talk their local language, and that can eliminate the suspicion that the students talk ill about the teacher.

Example:

When I was in South Africa as a high school teacher we used English as the official language teaching students. But the school had students from different regions and countries. Some students came from Kwazulu Natal province, Mpumalanga province and Gauteng province. Others came from Zanzibar, Malawi, Botswana and Kenya. The school was situated in Kwazulu Natal province where isiZulu, local language is mostly spoken. Almost all the students knew how to speak isiZulu language. As a teacher I was encouraged to know the language of isiZulu to get the benefits stipulated above. IsiZulu language helped me in class and in the province of Kwazulu Natal. Before coming to this school I was previously an Arabic teacher in the same province. As for many students, Arabic language was knew, English and isiZulu was commonly used to deliver lessons better in classes.

A Teacher Should Be Able To Use Examples

There are many times when things are not well understood. From the early years of a human being till today people may not understand some of the things which are said by other people. People tend to ask "what did he/she mean? Or what do you mean?" Failing to understand things has caused havoc in business, religion, education and caused distorted interpretation of the words. When a student does not understand what the teacher said there is high probability that the student will fail the exams.

The use of examples can somehow make things easy to understand, mostly in schools. Students have different understanding capability; others are quick to understand lessons while others are slow to understand lessons. A good teacher will use examples when delivering lessons to the students. He/she can give first example and ask the students if the point was understood. If he/she gets a feedback that the point was not understood, he/she can use a second example or more. To know if the point was understood, the teacher can ask questions or using his gesture will be able to know who did not understand the lesson. Examples used should be relevant to the topic and subject. The other important point to be careful with when giving example is that teacher should avoid giving sensitive examples that might offend students or the community the teacher lives, for example, teachers giving examples that offend other people's religion, race, sexual orientation and nationality. Although examples given can be true but no one would like to be used in negative examples. There are cases that a teacher was transferred or dismissed from work because of using offensive examples.

Example below was regarded as offensive example

In October, 2013 Jacob Zuma, the president of South Africa said: "We are in Johannesburg, this is Johannesburg. It's not some national road in Malawi". Zuma sparked controversy when he tried to convince motorist to accept the country's plan to toll highways around Johannesburg. Zuma's comments drew outrage across South Africa and Malawi, with social media platforms buzzing with ridicule and condemnation for the president's remarks. Malawians felt offended by his exemplification.

Although giving offensive examples should be avoided, there should be a consideration on academic freedom as it is important in education. Academic freedom is the freedom of teachers and students to teach, study, and pursue knowledge and research without unreasonable interference or restriction from law, institution regulations, or public pressure. Its basic elements include the freedom of teachers to inquire into any subject that evokes their intellectual concern, to present their findings to their students, colleagues, and others; to publish their data and conclusion without control or censorship; and to teach in the manner they consider professionally appropriate. For students, the basic elements include the freedom to study subjects that concern them and form conclusions and express their opinion.

Academic freedom and right of the students to know the truth are highly debatable issues. Questions may arise:

Will teaching history about brutality of apartheid system of government to black people in South Africa offensive to Afrikaners?

Will teaching how Hitler killed Jews be regarded as offensive?

If the above questions can be academic freedom and right to know, then what is offensive? If they are offensive topics, then what is academic freedom and right to know?

There is a requirement to balance between academic freedom and right of using offensive examples and topics. The balancing can be achieved using the following criteria:

- The academic freedom should benefit the society
- Tolerance to diversity should be practiced
- Academic freedom should be in accordance to law of the land
- People should accept the history and that truth should be told

GOVERNMENT LAWS AND ACADEMIC FREEDOM

In many countries teachers, students, and even college professors have faced intimidation and retaliation when they attempted to discuss scientific, political, economical critics of that particular country or an ally of that particular country. The assault on the academic freedom is bad to free society and to the progress of science, economy and politics, which depends on the robust debate and critical inquiry. It is entirely appropriate for the governments to ensure that teachers and students have right to freely discuss issues in an appropriate manner.

A case study of academic freedom in Malawi

Dr. Blessings Chinsinga was a Malawian lecturer at the centre of the Malawi Academic Freedom Standoff and eventual protest. He was a senior lecturer in Development Administration, Public policy Analysis and Institution, and development at university of Malawi Chancellor College. The standoff began when DR Chinsinga, who was an associate political science professor, was interrogated by Peter Mukhito, Malawi Inspector general of Police. In a political science lecture he had drawn comparisons that drew parallels between Malawi's fuel crisis and popular uprising in Tunisia and Egypt during the Arab spring. This comparison was reported to the police and he was eventually fired along with other lecturers such as Jessie Kabwila, Gaston Kanchedzera and Edge Kanyongolo.

This move received much criticism from the university and other organizations. It also prompted protests from UNIMA students that stood in solidarity with Chinsinga in support of academic freedom. The protest led to closure of Chancellor College and Polytechnic. It led to the involvement of then Minister of Education, Peter Mutharika and his brother President Bingu Mutharika. As a condition to return to class, the academics asked for an official apology from police chief, Mukhito and assurances of respect for academic freedom. The police chief declared that academic freedom had to be balanced because this was an issue of national security. This statement was supported by Bingu wa Mutharika who encouraged him not to apologize.

An academic freedom commission to solve the academic standoff was formed headed Brown Chimpamba. The register closed the two colleges of the university under the orders of the president in defiance of a court order that the lecturers had obtained. There was also a court order halting the dismissal of the staff and prevented the university from withholding salaries of the lecturers. The academic Standoff was one of the factors that led to the July 20, 2011 nationwide protest. Civil society was demanding the reinstatement of the professor and guarantee of academic freedom.

A TEACHER SHOULD BE ABLE TO ASK QUESTIONS

To find out whether a certain topic was understood, the teacher can ask learners questions. If more than 50 percent of the students answer it correctly that means that the topic was understood. If two-third of the students answered it wrong that means that the topic was not understood. A teacher can revise the topic using different tactics and methods. The teacher must also encourage students to ask questions from points which they did not understand. Students' questions can help the teacher to explain the topic more in detail.

When teachers prepare lessons they need to compose specific questions that they will ask students and/ or prepare to answer questions that students will ask them. Doing so will help teachers to increase students participation and encourage active learning. The strategies below will also help teachers to formulate questions for tests, assignments and examinations. Active learning extends beyond the classroom. When a teacher asks questions in the classroom, he/she is modeling a process that students should use themselves to develop their thinking skills and study. General strategies for asking questions are:

- When planning questions, a teacher should keep in mind his/her course goals. For example, does the teacher want students to master core concepts? Does the teacher want to develop students' critical thinking skills? The questions the teacher asks should help them practice these skills, as well as communicate to them the fact ideas, and ways of thinking that are important to the learning of the course.

- Avoid asking leading questions. A leading question is phrased in such a way that it suggests its own answer and therefore discourages students from thinking on their own.

- Follow a yes or no question with an additional question. For example, follow up by asking students to explain why they answered the way they did (yes/No), to provide evidence or an example.

- Aim for direct, clear, specific questions. During class discussion, rather than beginning with a single question that is multilayered and complex, use a sequence of questions to build depth and complexity. Essay questions on exams paper or assignments, on other hand, often provide an appropriate opportunity to ask multi-layered questions. If his/her exam will include multi-layered questions, the teacher should use questions during class time to walk students through the process of answering multi-layered questions.

- In class discussion, do not ask more than one question at once. When a teacher asks more than one question, students often do not respond because they are unsure which question the teacher wants them to answer.

- When the teacher plans each class session should include notes of when he/she will pause to ask and answer questions. Asking questions throughout the class will not only make the class more interactive, but also help the teacher to measure and improve students. Do not save the last two minutes of class for questions. Students are unlikely to ask questions when they know that only few minutes remain.

- Ask a mix of different types of questions. He/she should use "closed questions, or questions that have a limited number of correct answers, to test students' comprehension and retention of important information. He/she should also ask managerial questions to ensure, for example, that his/her students understand an assignment or have access to necessary materials. "Open questions, which prompt multiple and sometimes conflicting answers, are often the most effective in encouraging discussion and active learning in classroom.

- Wait for students to think and formulate responses. Waiting 5- 10 seconds will increase the number of students who volunteer to answer. If students do not volunteer before 5 seconds have passed, refrain from answering your own question, which will only communicate to students that if they do not answer, you will do their thinking for them. If students are unable to answer after sufficient time for thinking has passed, rephrase the question.

- Do not interrupt students' answers. You may find yourself wanting to interrupt because you think you know what the student is going to say, or simply because you are passionate about the material. Resist this temptation. Hearing the student's full responses will allow you to give them credit for their ideas and to determine when they have not yet understood the material.

- Show that you are interested in student's answers, whether right or wrong. Encourage students when they are offering answers by nodding looking at them, and using facial expression that shows you are listening and engage. Do not look down at your notes when they are speaking.

- Develop responses that keep students thinking. For example, ask the rest of the class to respond to an idea that one student has just presented, or ask the student who answered to explain the thinking that led to his/her answer.

- If a student answers an incorrect answer, point out what is incorrect or weak about the answer, but ask the student a follow – up question that will lead that student, and the class, to the correct or stronger answer.

The following are the main objectives of asking questions:

- To assess learning in progress/ or learning outcome
- To help the teacher to change method of teaching if the former was not understood
- To prompt students to explore attitudes, values, or feelings
- To prompt students to see a concept from another perspective
- To ask students to refine a statement or idea
- To prompt student to support their assertions and interpretation
- To direct students to respond to one another
- To prompt students to investigate a thought process
- To ask students to predict possible outcome
- To prompt students to connect and organize information

There are other ways of asking question, which are by the use of, quiz, tests, assignments and homework.

During quiz time the teacher should divide the class into groups, for example group A and group B. He/she should forward question to the first group and give them appropriate marks of their answer. If the group answers correctly the teacher can give the group 2 / 5/10 points, for example. Then the teacher can forward also the question to the other group and give it appropriate points. Quiz brings funny in the class and encourages different students to participate the interaction in class.

Besides the teacher asking questions the teacher can give opportunity to the students to formulate a number of questions for their group to ask the other group. This method of quiz encourages a sense of responsibility and encourages students to think.

The teacher can also formulate questions by giving students class test after the lesson, the week test, assignment and homework to help the students to be busy with the lesson. It also helps the teacher to find out areas that may need extra lesson or revision.

When a teacher give students tests and assignment should clear to the students on what he/she want students to do. The teacher should then mark tests and assignments of the students. Sometimes students are discouraged when their tests and assignments are not marked. They feel it a waste of time to write them because they will not be marked. Next time they will be reluctant to do any test and assignment that the teacher gives them.

The teacher should not teach less and depend only on homework and assignments. They should teach more and give less homework.

A Teacher Should Be Able To Prepare Examinations

In schools, examinations are used to find out if learners have understood what the teacher was teaching them after a certain period. It helps both the learners and the teachers. It is not only used to know how children have understood the lesson but also if the teacher has managed to teach children properly. The failure of the children can sometimes be because of the teacher did not teach the students properly or because the student's problem like slow learning, irregular attending of classes.

When the examination is out and the results shows there is a different grade of marks ranging from eighty percent going downwards, and that the half of the class has passed the examination, then the teacher has no any problem. The failing learners have individual problems. But if less than half of the class passed the examination and there are no higher marks, then the students never understood the lesson, the teacher may be a problem. To know a real course of poor performance of students a complete appraisal will be needed.

When setting examinations, a teacher must ask questions based on eighty percent of the work he/she taught because some students may be strong in other topics while others may be strong in other topics. If much of the work is been asked then the teacher is giving every student a chance to answer from what he/she knows best.

The teacher can use oral examination, written examination and/or practical examination. When the teacher conducts any examination he/she must try to put students at calm. Many students fear examinations and that can contribute to the failure of the students. Examination fever must be eliminated. Before exams the teacher should explain to the students what he/she wants from the examination. If it is a written paper a teacher must read to the students the entire paper before writing.

When setting examination papers, a teacher start with the simple questions and complete with the difficult questions. If the teacher starts with the difficult questions, it might cause the student to spend too much time in the question and sometimes he/she can lose the enthusiasm of examinations.

The teacher can divide the examinations into sections and differentiate the style of questions. Sections may include: multiple choice, fill the blank space, read the passage and answer the questions below, re-write the statement in the correct order, write brief statements of the following, case study, etc.

SAMPLE OF A SIMPLE QUESTION PAPER

ABUDARDA SECONDARY SCHOOL

2012   GRADE 10 FINAL EXAMINATIONS   140 Marks

Subject: BUSINES STUDIES   **Duration: IHR40**

Read the following instructions

Answer all questions

Write correct names

Use black or blue pen only

Understand the question before writing

Write neatly

Cheating is not tolerated

Section 1-Multiple Choice - Tick the correct answer
(15 marks)

1.1 _____ is a person who produces a good or service which he or she then sells in order to make money.
   (a) Marketer
   (b) Entrepreneur
   (c) Economist
   (d) Researcher

(3)

1.2 Costs that are not directly related to the level of production and do not change are
   (a) Fixed cost
   (b) Variable cost
   (c) Breakeven point
   (d) Income

(3)

1.3 The approach of generating new ideas where involves adapting old product is
   (a) the new-old approach
   (b) the new-new approach
   (c) SWOT analysis
   (d) Entrepreneurship

(3)

1.4 An agreement between two or more persons that is binding by law is called
   (a) Insurance
   (b) Contract
   (c) Business
   (d) United Nations

(3)

1.5 An example of fixed cost is
   (a) Depreciation
   (b) Raw material
   (c) Wages and salaries
   (d) Machine hours

(3)

Section 2 - Fill the blank space with a correct answer provided below   (15 marks)

[Minor, Hire-purchase agreement, Lease agreement, Insurance contracts, Employment.]

(1) An _____ contract is an agreement between the employer and the employee.

(3)

(2) An agreement in which one party promises to pay a sum of money to the other party upon the occurrence of a specific uncertain event in return for a sum of money is called _____

(3)

(3) _____ is a contract between the owner of the asset and the person who makes use of the asset.

(3)

(4) _____ is a contract between a customer and a business in which the business agrees to allow the customer to take possession of a good and the customer agrees to pay for the good in fixed installment over a given period of time.

(3)

(5) A _____ becomes a major when he or she is emancipated by his or her guardian.

(3)

Section 3- State whether the statements are true or false   (15 marks)

(1) Personal beliefs and prejudices also have profound effect on interpersonal relationship in the business environment.

(3)

(2) Discrimination can take place against religion

(3)

(3) Communication is the exchange of meaning

(3)

(4) In order to maximize profit, costs need to be maximized and revenue needs to be minimized

(3)

(5) The triple bottom line is a way of measuring a business's performance by considering three aspects of its operation.

(3)

Section 4- Choose the correct answer from the column B   (15 marks)

Column A	Column B
1. The process that allows one to make adjustments to the strategy if necessary	Management philosophy **Answer(1)** _____ **(3)**
2. It is the exchange of meaning	Environmental responsibility **Answer(2)** _____ **(3)**
3. The ideology and culture of the business as well as the style of management that is used in the organization	Stress **Answer(3)**_____ **(3)**
4.Business should produce as little waste and pollution as possible	Communication **Answer(4)**_____ **(3)**

5. It leads to exhaustion and inability to concentrate and deal with tasks effectively and ultimately affects your performance at work	Monitoring **Answer(5)**_____ **(3)**

Section 5 - Answer all questions   (80 marks)

(1)   Mention three characteristics of creative business environment   (6)

(2)   Explain what is forced combination technique   (3)

(3)   List three levels of management   (3)

(4)   What is co- ordination   (3)

(5)   What is a different of data and information   (4)

(6)   Explain economic return, social impact and environmental impact of the business   (6)

(7)   Mention three behaviors that can hinder team work   (6)

(8)   Mention three behaviors that can promote teamwork   (6)

(9)   What is business structure   (3)

(10) Mention two things that influence career choice   (4)

(11) Mention two factors that prevent effective problem solving   (4)

(12) Explain the following in the problem solving:

(a) identifying the problem (3)
(b) Strategy formulation (3)
(c) Monitoring (3)
(d) Evaluating (3)

(13) Explain SWOT analysis (6)

(14) Discuss five the general factors that (10)
entrepreneurs should keep in mind when
selecting a business location

(15) Explain why businesses use break – even (4)
analysis

The teacher must know where to position himself during examination when supervising the learners by not causing any tension and without giving students chance for discussions and using of text-books. He must be alert or spread his eyes to the whole class and not only interested in specific students.

Impartiality is recommended when marking the work of the students. The teacher should not favor a certain students because of the connections he has with the students. Students must be reminded that they must not only learn for examination but must learn to things.

After marking oral examination, written examinations and practical examination, a report should be issued. The report should contain information such as name of the student, grade, subjects, number of days absent, student's marks, position of the student, teachers/principal's comments, closing date, re-opening date, signatures, etc.

USING STUDENTS TO PRESENT LESSONS

When the teacher is teaching matured students can encourage them to present a lesson in manner of teaching other students. Student's presentation of the lesson can be done in different forms: students can present a lesson which was already taught. Using this form of presentation, the teacher can select students he wants to present the lesson. The other form is to give students a topic and areas where students will make research and present the lesson on a certain day. The teacher can divide the class into groups so that they will present the lesson in groups. While students present the lesson the teacher can make note of mistakes and correct them later. To encourage students' involvement, the teacher should give points / marks that can be added on marks of exams. Using students to present a lesson or certain information in the class audience has many advantages such as:

- It increases students to have interest on research
- It builds confidence in the hearts of the students
- It encourages hardworking of students
- It shows direct students' involvement in education
- It refreshes class environment

To continue encouraging the students, the teacher can use reward system to motivate students. A teacher should introduce rewards of different kind for the students' performance in the class. After the good performance from test, quiz, examination, etc, a teacher can give rewards in the like trophies, certificates, uniforms, etc in order to motivate students. The rewards also encourage poor performing students to do well and improve their performance.

Relationship Between Teachers and Students

Relationship between students and teachers need to be carefully encouraged because there is relationship that is important for the learning of the students and there is relationship that is detrimental to students. The relationship that is important to be encouraged in the school environment is the relationship that will enhance good learning environment which includes: mutual understanding between teachers and students. The mutual understanding will come up if students respect teachers, do the required exercises and other class work and when teachers do their job properly, helping students' class work and solving students' personal problems, exercising the love of parents, etc.

The detrimental relationship that may cause teachers to lose job and students lose school is the sexual relationship that may exist between teachers and students. There are so many teachers that lost job and others were jailed because of the sexual relationship existed between teachers and students. Although the large percentage of offenders are male teachers, there is a growing number of female teachers involved but cases are not taken seriously in many countries. The cases of sexual relationship are mostly found in higher classes where students reach puberty stage.

Teachers should avoid having sexual relationship with the students; they should regard them as their children. The impact is largely seen to female students. They lose school, and remain with the burden of looking after the children. Most of the time implicated teachers do not support the children born from the students. The root cause of sexual relationship varies: Some of the root causes are; regular talking about sex with students, use social media for charting with students/teachers, watching of pornographic materials, and regular visiting of students to teachers' houses, etc. Teachers should exercise self control all the time.

Teaching Aids

After explaining some qualities of the teacher, let us explain some of the teaching aids that help the teacher to teach effectively.

BOOKS

Books are some of the teaching aids teachers use. Books help teacher to prepare well lesson of the subject. The teacher uses books to information that makes it easy for him/her to execute knowledge to the students. A good teacher uses books as a source of reference, therefore he/she reads from different sources of books. Teachers should avoid using one book as source of reference as it may impact the quality of presenting a lesson in class. Although books are very important, teachers should not regard books as their substitutes where students are advised to learn on their own by using books. The teacher must teach and the books must support him, not the other way round.

Schools should provide relevant books to the teachers and students. The supply of books in developing countries' schools is limited comparing to developed countries. In the developed countries the students have more than one text books that they can use as a source of reference for the subject they learn. In the developing and underdeveloped countries is very hard to see students possessing text books for a number of subjects. Because of the limited books that students and teachers in the developing and underdeveloped countries possess, the quality of education is poor sometimes.

Choice of Books will depend on the grades/standards of the students and the curriculum used in the school. To use books that are irrelevant to the curriculum and syllabus will cost time and effort of students and teachers. The teachers should first look for the recommended books of the subjects. After getting the recommended books the teachers can search for additional reference books. The books that the teachers/students use should be books that are well written (wording and contents) so that they correspond to the level of students.

IMPORTANCE OF BOOKS TO STUDENTS

Books are very important in everyday life of the students because they are the source of information. The more books students read the higher the level of information students will get. Encouraging a love of books in toddlers is great way to make love school. It will also make them adapt to the concept of daily schoolwork. Books help them to learn new words and new ways of using the words that they already know. Reading books regularly stimulates children's imagination, accelerates their emotional development and fosters natural curiosity. Children quickly learn to visualize the scenarios mentioned in the stories by reading the text alone. Their knowledge on various subjects increases as children read different books. This can help them to become better students in school. Reading books improves a child's attention span. Books with colorful pictures work even better for young students than text only. Reading successfully replaces TV as a source of entertainment, especially if the child is introduced to preschool books as soon as he/she learns the alphabet.

Besides the books other teaching aids can be used, such as cards, charts, posters, etc. They can be placed on the wall where children can see them and make references.

Technology

Technology has definitely become a major influence in how people live. It has influenced systems of many organizations, and the way education systems operate. Technology has advanced with many advantages in the education system such as:

- Technology has made things easy for the teachers

Many things are perceived easy nowadays comparing with decade ago. With the invention of computers, printers, and other equipments has made school functions to be easy. If the teacher has a number of things to be printed or copied he/she can do it at his/her convenience without sending it to the printing/publishing houses. In so doing, teachers are able to deliver the lesson faster than in decades ago.

- Reduction of material and time cost

The technology influenced the reduction of material and time cost in schools. For example when a teacher does not want to use papers he/she can use the overhead projector to teach students. The lesson that could have used hundreds of papers to give students, the teacher can use the projector and computer to deliver the lesson. It is also faster to use projector than only board. The contents that can be covered using the projector and computer are much greater than the use of board only.

- Information research on the tip of the figure

Comparing to the decades ago researching information was cumbersome. It needed people to buy books or go to library and search information page by page. With the event of technology, a teacher can get information while seating at home. Just the use of internet he/she can visit various websites and e-libraries that provide credible information. In addition, in most higher education institutions, where there is advancement of technology, students are provided with devices that contains all books, and other learning materials. A student or a teacher can only take the laptop or any other device like flash disks, CDs and others.

- E- Learning

The distance of learning is made easy by the use e-learning. Distance learning in the past decades was cumbersome. To receive learning materials took a long period of time. In the process other materials got lost. With the e-Learning a student can get the information by the use of internet. Teachers in the e-learning can teach using the internet. Students by using computers and internet can connect with their teachers and follow the lessons that can be similar to students learning using tradition system in the classroom.

DISADVANTAGES OF TECHNOLOGY

Although technology has brought a number of benefits in the education systems, there are also some disadvantages that emerge because of it. Some of them are:

- Health hazard

The use of computers and headphones contribute to the danger of the health of the person. The constant using of computers may cause eyes problems and the regular use of headphones/earphones may have implications to ear drum. If the teacher experiences eye or ear problem will find it difficult to communicate with his students. The teacher might not be able to see properly in class or fail to read properly when preparing lessons. In the event of marking assignment and exams the teacher can mark correct answers wrong because of the eye problem.

- Increase of social media in class

The booming of the use social media among the youth is disturbing classes. Students use Facebook and Whats-up to chat with their friends while they are in class. The use of social media by students in class has impacted the quality of education of many students because students cannot understand the lessons taught by the teacher in class.

Although students are in the forefront in the use of social media, a number of teachers also use social networks in class which also has an impact to deliver good lessons.

- Internet information not 100% correct

Although there is abundance of information in the internet, teachers should be careful when getting information. Not all information in the internet is 100% correct; therefore the teacher should visit websites that are trustable.

- Maintenance cost

The introduction of technology has increased the number of equipments that are used in school. The increase of equipments in school has increased the maintenance cost for example, repairing the broken equipments.

- Brain loafing

The regular use of technological equipment like the calculator in mathematics, can cause brain loafing. The teacher should encourage the students to use brain (mental arithmetic) when solving simple mathematics to reduce brain loafing.

EQUIPMENTS USED IN SCHOOL

Teachers use TVs, DVDs and videos to show students something important for the lesson. For example, teachers can show students earthquakes, volcanoes, tornadoes and tsunamis, etc as a support to the lesson. Before commencing the show to the teacher should provide a summary of the show. The teacher should ask the students to take notes while viewing the show. When the show is over the teacher should ask questions or let them ask questions on things that they need more clarification.

The other equipment that can be used by a teacher is a projector. It helps the teachers to deliver the lessons by using computer programs such as the PowerPoint, Excel, Word, etc. In addition, teachers can use microphones and loud speakers when they are delivering lessons to the larger audience.

Science teachers use lab equipments to carry out different tests of chemistry, biology, and other scientific subjects. Calculators can also be used by Science and Mathematics teachers when solving mathematical and other scientific problems.

School Environment

No school can survive without considering the environment it operates. The school environment impacts the performance of the school. The school environment can be classified into internal environment and external environment. The internal environment is the environment that is found in the school and the management has direct control over it. The external environment is the environment that exist outside the school and the management has no direct control over it

INTERNAL SCHOOL ENVIRONMENT

School internal environment consist of the goals, objectives, teachers, students, classrooms, registration system, school departments, school culture, laboratory, computer rooms, playing grounds, etc.

TEACHERS

Teachers are the fundamental pillars of the school. The mixing of the teachers between the old and the young put the school environment in the right position. Good teachers are the ones that even if they are old enjoy executing lessons to students. Young teachers can gain experience from them. Mutual relationship between the old and the young teachers will encourage old teachers to train young teachers and transfer their competences for the success of the school. Good understanding and respect among teachers bring good school environment.

To continue having good school environment, stability of teachers is very important. The stability of teachers brings stability of culture and core competences of the school. It helps the school to continue having quality students and high performance. Lack of stability of teachers affects the quality of education at the school. The departure of teachers confuses and demoralizes the students because students relationship with teachers is not build over night. Once the relationship is built, it is not necessary to break it before the end of the year. For the students to build another relationship with the new teacher takes also a number of days. In the process of building relationship with the new teachers, time is lost.

STUDENTS

Students are the pillars of schools. There is no school in the world that can exist in the absence of the students. Enrolling good number of students is an important element for the success of the school. Effective utilization of the school will be attained when the school enrolls a big number of students necessary to its effective capacity. For example, the school that has 500 students as maximum capacity may be regarded as effective capacity utilization when it enrolls 400-500 students.

Failing to utilize effectively the capacity of the school, cost of running the school may be high with minimum positive results. Some schools were closed because of small number of students they had at the school. The other importance of the students is their position as a source of evaluating performance of the teachers and the school. The performance of the teachers and school is evaluated using the performance of the students. The school is regarded as highly performing school when students of the school are highly performing and the school is regarded as poor performing school when students perform badly.

To have good performance of the school will depend on various factors that help to produce good results: The school environment, quality teachers, availability of resources and the quality of students. Students' attitude towards school may influence the quality of education at school. If the school has large number of students who have apathy and rudeness attitude will negatively impact the performance of the teachers and the school. Issues of students have been explored in detail below under students' chapter.

CLASS ROOMS

As mentioned previously, many parents and grand-parents were taught under trees without classrooms and books. During the time of rain and heavy wind the classes were interrupted. In the developing world, many areas still experience shortage of classrooms. Some of the classrooms in the developing world are built using muddy bricks which are not strong and sometimes cause injuries and death when the classrooms fall during rainy and windy seasons. The teachers teaching in bad classrooms like these are mostly affected by the conditions of the classrooms while teachers teaching in good classrooms are not affected and their performance may be high.

Safety is an important factor to consider when teaching students. If the teacher fears any danger, for instance a collapsing roof or a falling wall, it is better to stop teaching in that classroom and conduct lessons outside while waiting for the classroom to be fixed. A classroom must look pleasant, clean; have good ventilation that allows sufficient light and air to enter. Lack of sufficient light can cause eye problems to the teachers and students. Unclean or unhygienic classrooms can cause diseases to the teachers and the students which can influence their performance. If there are no supporting staffs like cleaners to clean the classrooms, the teacher can appoint volunteers from the learners to clean the classroom on rotation basis.

REGISTRATION

Registration of students in many schools begins towards the end of the term/year. The registration should be done in accordance to the strategy and objectives of the school. For example if the goal of the school is to produce best students in Science subjects then in the time of registration the school will register only those students that are capable to produce best results in Science. If the school's objective is to increase the literacy level in the community, then registration will not be strict comparing to the school that is pursuing objectives of producing best Mathematics or Science students.

Before registration, authorities should consider the classrooms, number of teachers, financial capability of the school. It is not good to enroll hundred students per class while the classroom can only accommodate thirty students. If the school enrolls big number of students more than its capacity a number of problems can emerge. The school can face shortage of resources; there can be increase of spread of diseases due to the big number of students in one class.

The ability of a teacher must be taken seriously. If the number registered students is more than what he/she can handle or is capable of teaching he/she will not be able to deliver the lessons effectively. A good number of students that teacher can effectively handle is between 30 - 45 students in one class. The standard number of students will enable the teacher to handle the class properly.

Enrolling a large number of students while the school cannot afford to increase the number of teachers will jeopardize the quality of education at the school.

The budget is also the most important aspect when running schools. Schools fail to function properly because of the insufficient money available to run the schools. Many teachers sometimes stop teaching when they fail to get their monthly salary or when the salary is not enough comparing to the increase of living cost in many countries. When formulating school budget, cost of books, teaching materials, maintenance should be included.

When all school preparations and budget of the year is formed, the registration of learners should start. Forms must be issued to the parents who want their children to learn at the schools. The form should include the following school and student's information:

- School information: name, address and contact details of the school, rules and regulations of the school, name and signature of the head teacher (Headmaster/ School Principal), date, etc.
- Student's information: name, address and contact details of the student, grade/ standard, gender, age, health problems, criminal record, hobbies, sporting activities that he/she plays, fees, disabilities, signature of the student, signature of the parent/ or guardian, etc.

REGISTRATION FORM SAMPLE

Orient Hill Secondary School
45 Citrus Drive
Isipingo 4115
Tel: 0027313034788

Date_____

Registration Form

Class/Grade applying for _____
FIRST NAME _____ SURNAME _____
DISTRICT /Town coming from _____
ADRESS: _____
_____
_____
Next of Kin 1 _____ Address _____
_____
_____
Cell _____
Email_____
Next of Kin 2 _____ Address _____
Cell _____
E mail_____
Do you suffer from any disease that needs a special care?
Yes/No _____
If yes provide the details _____
what criminal record do you have? _____

Hobbies: 1 _____ 2 _____
Skills: 1_____ 2_____

```
Oath: I

_____

shall abide by the rules and regulations of the school and
shall accept the punishment applied by the school if I
may be found guilty.


Student's signature _____
School representative sign_____
```

When the school opens for the first term, children should be welcomed by the head teacher on the general assembly and class teacher in the class. When welcoming students in the general assembly, the head teacher should put the tone of why the school is the pleasant place to be by informing students all pleasant programs school planned for the students, like, sports, excursion trips, funny days, etc. After the pleasant information is mentioned the head teacher should emphasize the importance of education and the vision of the school in terms of education. The head teacher should put explain how he/she wants the school to produce best results on that particular year. Then, the principal should lay down rules and regulations of the school. The head teacher should show how discipline is taken seriously at the school and what kind of punishment is used when the student is found guilty.

In the class, the teacher should introduce his name and let also the students introduce their names. After the class introduction the teacher can tell the students about the surroundings of the school like toilets and grounds. The class teacher should expand from what the head teacher said on the assembly on areas of importance of education and discipline. Children must be reminded about all information signed in the form, namely, the rules, conduct, times, subjects and punishment for breaking school rules.

All names registered for the school must be recorded in the books. Forms must be kept in a safe place. It is credible for the teacher to have a register book which he/she can use to call out names of students every day in the class. The register will help the teacher to have an insight on the conduct of the students. The teacher will be able to assess students that frequently miss classes. If the students frequently miss classes, the teacher should investigate the main reasons of the absence of the students. Some of the reasons that cause students to absent from classes are: sickness, family problems, financial problems, apathy, etc. To improve the conduct of the learners the school can introduce incentives and these may range gifts, certificates and trophies.

LABORATORY

The teachers of Science subjects need laboratories to enable them to teach students properly. Science subjects become very difficult for the teachers to teach if there are no laboratories. There are certain topics that require practice and experiment. Students cannot understand the subjects by the use of theories only.

A lot of schools in the developing counties do not have laboratories which impact to the number of students graduated in the fields of sciences. Most of the schools fail to have laboratories because of the buying and maintenance cost. To reduce the problem schools can have partnership on the laboratory. Four to five schools can agree to have one laboratory where schools can use it in rotation. The schools number of days one school can use before the other. The school partnership can ease the problem of the laboratory and help the students that pursue science subjects to pass with high marks.

The laboratory should be equipped with apparatus to function effectively. There is no use to have a building designated for the laboratory but there is insufficient equipment to use.

COMPUTER ROOM

The world is changing almost every day. One of the contributing factors to change is the event of technology. Most of businesses nowadays use computers to process work. The need for computer literacy has increased the demand to teach students computers at early age. The pressure is on the schools to have computer rooms where students can learn how to use computers.

The introduction of computer classes in schools has opened a need to employ computer or Information Technology (IT) teachers. Schools that have the ability to have computer rooms should emphasize on the quality of teachers that will be able to teach students computers. Schools should not only consider IT teachers and financial status when introducing computer classes but also the number of students.

Schools if they are capable can separate computer rooms for junior and senior students. Schools that can only afford one computer room should allocate time for junior and senior students. Schools that cannot afford to have a computer room can jointly have one computer room with partner schools and use in rotation. In this situation only the senior students can be considered.

SCHOOL CULTURE

Different schools have different culture. School culture is very important because it gives identity of the school. The most distinct forms of school culture are:

- **School uniforms**: A school uniform is very important for the school. It is an identity of the school. In the event of accident people are able to identify where the students learn their school.

School uniform provides equality between the poor and the rich. It reduces pride of some rich people. The equality of students can help teachers to look at the students equally. School uniform beautifies the school.

- **School reports:** School reports provide the summary of the performance of the students in schools. The design and contents of the school report may be different. Other schools provide reports that contain results of all school terms on one sheet while others provide one term results.

School reports are very important as they give the teachers, students, parents and school an outlook of the performance level of the students. Teachers or schools that fail to provide school reports, leave parents in doubt about the progress of the child.

- **School holidays:** School holidays are very important for the teachers, students, schools and parents. Teachers and students will have time to rest teaching and learning respectively. Parents will also get rest on preparing students to school. Schools will have time to evaluate the activities of education at the school. Schools enjoy school holidays differently. In other countries school holidays are conducted 3 times a year while others conduct 4 times a year. Religious schools have also different school holidays.

- **Language:** Schools chose languages to use at schools as medium of communication. The choice of languages is influenced by government policies and school objectives. Other schools may emphasize local languages to be used in schools so that students are able to understand the lessons easily than teaching them in foreign languages. Other schools may emphasize foreign languages like English, Arabic, and French, to equip students for international market.

- **School time**: School working hours is mostly influenced by the government policies, religious bodies and communities. Governments may implement policies of school working hours to influence the education in the country. The government can increase school hours from 5 hours to 8 hours so that teachers will have enough time to deliver lessons. Religious schools may also have their school working hours that are fit for their religious activities. Sometimes because of larger number of students, schools may divide students into two sessions. One group of students may come in the morning hours while the other group of students may come in the afternoon.

SCHOOL STRUCTURE

Traditionally hierarchy of school involves headmaster (headmistress)/principal as the head of the school. His responsibilities are to manage the affairs of the school. He/she is the chief commander of the school, all teachers and students take his/her orders. He/she performs an interpersonal role with the outside organizations, for example, meetings with union, community members, and government representatives. He/she is accountable to the government, executive board of the school. The principal may have a vice or deputy principal of the school. He/she is given certain duties to carry out on behalf the principal. However the principal provide final decisions on all matters of the school. Most of the time principals and vice principals are former teachers who worked in education for a good number of years.

The principal's office is assisted by the secretary of the school or principal's secretary. The principal appoints heads of departments who are responsible to run their departments competitively. They ensure that their departments are managed well on all academic issues at the school. Given below is a sample of simple school structure.

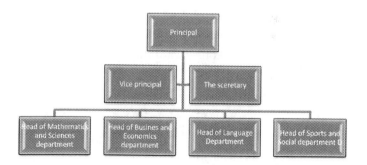

PLAYING GROUND

Playing grounds at the school burnishes good school environment. The school planners should provide space where sports activities can take place. There are a number of sporting activities in the world. A number of sporting activities are different country to country. Example of sporting activities that schools can use may include soccer, rugby, cricket, hockey, volleyball, basketball, marathon, jumping, tennis, etc. What is astonishing is that a number of schools do not have even a single ground where students can play. Furthermore, the locations and neighborhoods where a number of students come from do not have good grounds. With the rampant construction works in some cities and countries planners overlook the need of parks and playing grounds for the children. Children do not have grounds to play. When children come home from school, they only play with TV games, which do not give them any physical benefit. The lack of playing grounds in schools and neighborhoods is a significant factor that causes students to engage in things such smoking cigarettes, drinking alcohol, smoking drugs, fighting and other immoral issues.

Safety is another parents' concern in schools where playing grounds are provided. Sometimes parents wish to see their children participating in sporting activities but the fear is the safety of children from crime and influence of bad friends. In other schools students are abducted, intimidated and killed. Parents are confused whether to send their children to play or not. Therefore schools and teachers should value safety of students in playing grounds. The schools and neighborhoods should take ground safety seriously. To take safety measures seriously, schools can allocate time when each class can use the grounds. When the students are out for sports, a sports supervisor or teacher should be present to control students and the sports. The problem is when the supervisor or sports teacher is not available at the grounds; students cannot manage to control themselves when violence starts.

Sport is good for the body. Students become fit and strong. It can help students to have good blood circulation, which can make help them to improve their performance in class. When the child grows older, his body stays fit compared to one who do not play or participate in any sporting activity. Teachers can join students in the ground as a form of students' motivation.

The introduction of sports in schools keeps children busy rather than spending time in useless things. It encourages friendship, understanding and helping among the students if well managed.

EXCURSION

Learning does not end in the class only. Students can have learning trip which can help them to learn various things. Taking students for excursion is very important. During the trip students experience wonderful things that is not available in their schools or locations. Some students when they come back from excursion decide to change their careers to the careers they saw during the excursion. For example, when students go to media houses, business places, factories, airports, mining, hospitals, prefer to be like people in those places.

Excursion gives true experience of things like mountains, sea, dangerous animals, new places, buildings, roads, factories and many more sights. In other lessons teachers might teach students something which will be well understood only when they see the thing. Such experiences can give the students interest of learning more or pursuing a career that will help them in the future.

Excursions should be well prepared. Bad and dangerous places should not be an option places for the trip. Places like casinos, pubs, are not good for the excursion. It is not good to take students to places that will encourage them to do wrong things and lead them to choose bad career. Before taking students for excursions, the teacher should ask parents to sign the indemnity forms which give teachers right to take students for excursions. Teachers can ask two or more parents to accompany them on excursions so that they can help teachers controlling the students.

If the school does not have money for excursion, parents of the students can be asked to contribute money towards the trip. The budget must include transport and food. Booking of the venue or place where the excursion is being planned for must be done in advance to have assurance of the place because the place might allow other people and turn you back because of the limited space available. Early planning saves time, money and bolsters confidence.

Transport should be booked in advance to avoid problems. The organizers must choose the transport that is roadworthy. Safety of students should be given priority. Some trip organizers are not honest; they like to take some money from the trip budget and use it for personal reasons and shun from taking a good vehicle for the trip. Once they take money from the budgeted money funds becomes insufficient and get bad vehicle for the trip. The bad vehicle may cause accident and a lot of students and teachers may die.

Teachers should register all students going for the trip and count them when leaving and returning from the trip. Students should be reminded for the good behavior and dressing code. It gives schools bad image if the students do not behave well. School uniform is the best dressing code during the trip.

Teachers should guard students and prevent any problem which may occur during the trip. Students who have diet problems should be noted and special meal for them should be prepared. If there a lot of students, teachers should group them for better security and easy distribution of food.

SPECIFIC SCHOOL ENVIRONMENT

Specific school environment is the environment of the school after the internal environment and the school teachers or authorities do not have control over it but they can influence it for the benefit of the school. In this environment there are teachers' unions, parents, sponsors, and the communities.

TEACHERS' UNION

Teachers' union is an organized labor union of teachers that represent them to the employers (government) on issues that concern them such as condition of work, salary increase, policy change, etc. Teachers' union is financed by monthly member contributions. If the negotiation with government fails teachers' union may call for a strike or a standoff.

Benefits teachers get from teachers' union

- Teachers' union brings unity among the teachers and makes them speak with one voice
- The concerns of teachers are taken seriously by the government comparing to concerns that can be tabled individually.
- There will be uniformity in the event of increase of salaries; conditions of work and therefore no one feels de-motivated.

Impacts of teachers' union to school environment

- Teachers have to attend teachers' union meeting during class time which impacts delivery of lessons.
- Teachers' union concentrate only what is good for the teachers but not the students.
- Governments may fail to implement important policies for the benefit of the education because teachers' union may oppose them.
- Teachers' union may call for a strike/ standoff which impact classes and sometimes examinations.

Recognition of teachers' union varies country to country. Other countries recognize teachers' union while others don't. During the strike head teacher may influence the teachers at the school but cannot control issues that concern the union.

PARENTS

Parents are the vital player of school environment. They are the ones that choose school for their children. If the school has good relationship with parents, school benefits a lot. Some of the benefits are:

- Increased number of students.
- Parents' involvement on school activities.
- Parents contribute easily financials requirements of the school.
- Parents influence good behavior of students to the teachers.

The school that has no good relationship with the parents of the students faces tremendous problems, such as:

- Parents may take their children out of the school.
- Parents may be on the side of the student even if the student is wrong.
- Parents may not cooperate to attend important meetings of the school.
- Parents may not send their children to important activities of the school, such as sports, excursions competitions, etc.

The teacher and the school should introduce parents' involvement system at the school. Teachers can have one on one meeting with parents of his/her students at a certain day where both parents and teachers evaluate the performance of the students and find ways of improving the performance; or the teacher/principal can call parents meeting on one of the weekend and get parents' ideas on the progress, challenges and improvements of the school. The principal can call the meeting once a month or after every three months.

SPONSORS

For the school to function properly requires sponsors. Sponsors of the school can be categories into two: student sponsors and school sponsors.

STUDENT SPONSORS

These are sponsors who sponsor students. They are can be organizations or individual sponsors. They help students with school fees, school uniforms, stationeries, scholarships, etc. They help the vulnerable students who are coming from the poor families. Other sponsors give money to the students to buy required things themselves while others prefer to buy needed items for the students and distribute them to the students.

Sponsors get names of the poor students at the school on the approval of the head teacher. When sponsors come to school to get names of poor students head teachers should not bias for or bias against any student. The head teachers should give the appropriate information so that the intended benefits reach the responsible people. And confidentiality should be observed to avoid embarrassing the sponsored students.

Good relationship between the sponsors and the schools/teachers should be maintained so that students continue benefiting from the sponsorship. If the relationship is poor, sponsors may retract their sponsorship from the students at the school and give it to other students in different school. Sometimes sponsors may influence the sponsored students to stop learning at the school and go to other schools if they want to continue with the sponsorship.

Other schools/ teachers do not allow sponsorship of the students because of the sponsorship is coming from a different religious group. Failing to accept the students at the school because he/she is receiving the sponsorship from the different religious group can be regarded as discrimination in other countries.

If there is good relationship between school and the students sponsors, students may not be turned back from school because of the delay of the fees as the school has guarantee that the fees will be paid.

SCHOOL SPONSORS

These are sponsors who support schools. Supporting schools with donations of assets such as computers, desks, printers, photocopy machines, etc; donation of money; building of classrooms; donation of laboratories, libraries, etc. The sponsorship can come from the organizations or the individual persons. Sponsors get the names of schools from the governments or receive letters from schools asking for assistance or sponsors can conduct a research to find the poor schools.

Head teacher should be active looking for sponsorship of the school and students. The school should make sure that there is good relationship between the school and the sponsor. A poor relationship with the school may result into diverting the sponsorship to the other schools.

To increase the relationship the principal should have regular meetings with the sponsors or should introduce involvement systems like suggestion schemes. Although politics, religions influence receipt of sponsorship by other organizations, the principal should not accept or deny the sponsorship on the basis of political or religious reason as long as the sponsorship does not have bad preconditions.

MACRO SCHOOL ENVIRONMENT

Macro school environment is the environment of the school which principals, teachers do not have control over it. The main influencing factors in this environment are politics, economy, social and technology. PEST analysis is the tool that provides in-depth analysis of how the external environment of the school will look like, and provides opportunity for school management to select good strategies.

POLITICAL ENVIRONMENT

The political environment consist the changes of governments, regulations and policies. Some of the effects that political environment could have on the school are:

- **School being privatized**

The government can decide to privatize the school that was previously run by the government. The new owners of the school will have a different objective of running the school. Their main objective will be profit maximization. The new owners of the school can change the principal, the teachers and the school culture. The change can either be positive or negative to the school, teachers, principal and others.

- **Changes to the skills required to be a teacher**

The government can change the requirements for a person to be a teacher. The government can introduce new requirements after the analysis of the changing environment. The requirements may include changes of qualifications needed, the minimum age to be a teacher, the retiring age of the teacher, financial skills requirements to a principal.

When there is scarce of teachers governments tend to employ teachers without necessary skills but when there is an increase of teachers governments tend to be strict on total quality of the teacher. A good teacher is the one who continuously improve his/her skills to meet the changing environment.

- **Changes to curriculum**

The government can decide to change the curriculum of the schools because of its irrelevance to the changing environment to solve the needs of the country. The new curriculum may make other subjects and topics obsolete and bring in new subjects and topics that are relevant.

The implementation of the new curriculum might be difficult to other teachers. When the new curriculum is introduced governments introduce new systems to implement the curriculum. The new systems might not be compatible to the capabilities of teachers therefore the desired output is not achieved.

- **Requirement to be self financing**

Governments can decide to withdraw a portion of funding schools. For example, the governments may reduce the funds they give per students from $10 to $5. The reduction will stretch the funding of the schools. The schools may decide to increase the school fees which eventually affect the poor families and cause their children to drop school. The reduction of governments funding per student may cause shortfalls of finances at schools to pay teachers and other running costs.

ECONOMIC ENVIRONMENT

This environment is concerned with the economic issues of people, schools, and the country. The economic factors can influence positively or negatively to the functions of the school. The school cannot control the economic environment but economic environment can force the school to change the way it function so that it adapts to the environment. The following are some of the economic factors that influence school environment.

- **Closure of a local industry may affect fund raising plans of the school**

Many schools do not relay only governments for the finances of the school but they spread their fundraising plans to local industries. The closure of the local industries will impact the finances of the school. The school is then forced to look for companies that are outside the location. Failing to get the potential financer for the school will force schools to cut some functions.

- **Ability of parents to raise funds for optional activities**

Other activities of the school are not budgeted in the school budget. The school may only budget for the essential activities and exclude excursion, sports, and other activities. The school may request the parents to funding the unbudgeted activities. If the financial status of many parents is good will be able to contribute to the school but if the financial status of many parents is poor due to unemployment will not be able to contribute to the school activities. Failure of parents to fund the school will cause austerity measures to be implemented by the school management.

- **Cost of resources**

The rising cost of resources of the school such as teachers, equipments (Computers, printers, copier machines, etc), books, papers, etc can have a negative impact to the school. There will be acute shortage of resources because of the rising cost. However, the decline cost of resources will help the school to have enough resources and improve the quality of education at the school.

- **Interest rate**

When the interest is increased, schools that depend on borrowing banks money will not be able to borrow the required amount because of the high interest rate. Interest rate is the percentage that banks charge over the borrowed money. Government central banks decide to increase or decrease the interest rate. It is used in the monetary policy of the government. High interest rate can be used to decrease the buying power of the consumers in order to avoid high inflation rate. People/ businesses are discouraged to borrow money from the bank. The government can reduce the interest rate to increase the buying power of the consumers. People/ businesses are encouraged to borrow money from the bank.

- **Shortages of material on national markets**

Resource is one of the important factors for a successful school. If the school is lacking necessary resources, the quality of teaching and education will be jeopardized. If the country is facing the shortage of resources for schools such as papers, computers, books, the country is forced to import the books from other countries. The exchange rate is considered when importing things from outside the country. If the exchange rate of the country is high, the country or the school will spend a lot of money on few items. Besides the exchange rate, delivery time is another negative factor of importing things from other countries.

- **The risk of losing highly valued staff members**

Employees have different interests at the work but the most common interest of workers at the work place is to salaries or wages. People compare their efforts with amount of reward they receive. In the time of high cost of leaving people put money first as their number one priority at the work place. If other schools are open with high paying system than their schools, the schools can lose high skilled teachers to their competitors. The departure of highly skilled teachers affects school culture and quality of education. The school can also lose students because of the loyalty other students might have with teachers.

SOCIAL ENVIRONMENT

Social environment involves changes in the nature and norms of the society. Demography of population can change. Key demographic factors include: growth rate, changes in the wealth of people, changes in the house hold and family structure, changes in the culture, behavior and attitudes of people.

- **Declining in birth rate, reflecting national trend**

There are many factors that influence the decline of birth rate. Some of them are: career advancement of men and women where they decide to have children after finishing their studies; responding to birth control campaign where families are advised to control number of children. The decline of birth rate might have negative impact to the school. The decline of children born will result to decline of the students' population at schools. In other circumstances schools close down due to insufficient number of students; or school management might reduce the number of teachers employed by the school.

- **Local population changes**

Population density is one factor to consider when analyzing the future of the school. The population of the area can increase or decrease depending on a number of factors such as increase or decrease of factories, urbanization, land fertility, availability of resources, etc. The place that faces high level of factory openings will experience increase of population therefore the demand of social services like health centers and schools will increase. If there is existing schools, the increase of population will require the schools to increase the number of classes, school teachers and other facilities. In contrast the decrease of population in the community where the school operates will negatively impact the school. The number of students will decrease and consequently the school might close down or reduce the teaching staff.

- **Changes to qualifications requirements**

Due to the changing environment, qualifications may become obsolescent. Therefore government may introduce a certain level of qualification for a qualified teacher. The government may also change the name of the qualifications. If the school has teachers whose qualifications are affected by the new law should be advised and supported to get new qualifications. The school can send teachers to workshops, seminars, colleges, universities to study more so that they meet requirements of the government.

Integration of students with special needs with other normal students

Students with special needs are students that have physical problems like blindness, deaf, dumb, and other physical problems. Although it is advisable to educate them in their own schools so that special teachers and facilities can be easily allocated for them, the government can plan to integrate them with other students because of insufficient number of schools that carter for students with special needs. Integrating them with normal students has many advantages. Some of them are: It reduces discrimination; students accept and learn that students with special needs are also like them; students with special needs feel motivated as they feel that they are part of the world; schools get good image and publicity.

When the school integrate students with special needs extra resources will be required for students with special needs. Teachers will need to be trained on how to handle students with special needs.

TECHNOLOGICAL ENVIRONMENT

Technological environment include three aspects: equipments, the method of using that equipments, and the organizational requirements of using the equipments. These days we tend to use the term 'technology' to imply some computer applications, but in its widest sense we should be considering all types of equipments, systems and procedures. Changes in the technological environment can impact directly on an organization's ability to carry out its objectives. Improvements in machine capability, the systems employed or the way the organization uses that machinery can, for example reduce costs or improve the way in which a service is delivered. The technological environment is complex and dynamic. Organizations find it difficult to plan effectively in such unstable conditions where new developments can revolutionize the way in which operations are carried out very quickly. Technology has enabled greater access to information for decision-making purposes, both from within the organization and outside it. Management information systems and decision support systems take data from that already available within the company and re-present it in a format that managers can use to aid decision-making. There is an improvement in communications: for example, networking of PCs, video conferencing, and mobile phones. Technology environment has various impacts to school, such as:

- **New computer virus may harm school operations**

Computers play a big a role in the schools. It is used for typing, formulating and analyzing of information for the schools. But the negative impact of computers is the computer virus. Every year there is a new virus that is innovated to corrupt the computers. The virus affects school operations. The computers virus can cause the computers to crash, slow down the operations and/or corrupt the important information.

- **Distributing illegal images on the internet may affect ICT security measures**

There is ethical concern in the use of computers and internet. Is the use of computers by teachers for personal use regarded as unethical? Should teachers use school computers when they want to send very important e-mails to their spouses? Schools should provide guidelines on the use of computers by teachers to clear the problems on ethical issues.

The use of internet in schools has brought a number of challenges. Some teachers and students browse websites that distribute pornographic materials. Pornographic materials can become apparent in school computers if they are not well secured. Besides using computers some students and teachers use cell phones to browse immoral websites.

The rising of pornography in schools has negatively impacted the environment of the school. Immoral activities happen in schools and the surrounding places. There are incidences where teachers give students pregnancy; or students raping female teachers. The impact is that when a teacher impregnates student then the student losses school and the teacher loses job and face criminal charges. The school will be affected from bad publicity and dented image and students lose class time. All these immoral acts are rising because of viewing and distributing pornographic material and other immoral materials.

MOVE FROM PAPER BASED BOOKS TO E-BOOK READERS

Technology has simplified a number of things. The tradition way of learning is gradually diminishing. There is an increase of e-learning in different schools, mostly in colleges and universities. The departure from paper based books to e –books has some positives and negatives. Some of the positives are:

- E-book can be copied to a friend at a click of a button while the paper book can take days
- In e- book, the size of numbers and letters can be changed any time to fit the requirements of the user while paper book can not

- It is easy to carry. A number of books can be saved in a small device, for example, 4GB flash/ USB.

SOME OF THE DRAWBACKS OF E- BOOKS ARE:

- Computer virus can corrupt the books
- Excessive use of e-book affects the eyes
- It's easy to lose the e-books by wrongfully touching the delete button
- Books are lost when the person lose a device which contains the books.

When the school decides to move from paper based books to e-books should evaluate the benefits and negative impact the e-book can have to the school. The analysis should include the knowledge base of the teachers and students to understand if they know how to use the e-book. The cost of implementing the new system in terms of procurement cost, maintenance cost, training cost should be considered.

Old practices can infringe the implementation of the new practices. The attitude of the users is another factor as many senior people would find it difficult to change to new system. The school then can implement the system after greater consultation with the users of the new system.

- **Computer hard ware being out of date**

Technology environment is changing every day. There are new computers, systems, and processes that are coming up every day. The life span of computers is not a very long life span; therefore the computers become out of date after the end of its life span. When the computer is outdated, the system fail to function properly, the computer becomes slow, regular problems with hardware and software of computers. The school or the teachers become negatively affected by the performance of the computers. Work cannot be done at a faster pace, information may be lost, and cost of maintenance can be high.

- **ICT systems management**

Managing ICT system is a vital activity in the technology environment. Failing to manage ICT properly might result to the increase of maintenance cost, abuse of system, rising insecurity from hackers and unethical issues shared in the internet. Many schools face numerous challenges to manage ICT systems. The main problem is that many schools do not have specialist who can manage the ICT system. Many schools with computers assign a teacher to monitor that the students are not abusing the computers but he/she may not have good skills and knowledge of managing ICT. The main reason of many schools to fail having ICT qualified person is the lack of resources to pay a qualified person to manage the ICT system of the school.

LEGISLATIVE ENVIRONMENT

Legal environment is the environment that deals with the laws and regulations of the country that are aimed to control and protect the country from ill- discipline of people and organizations so that appropriate actions can be taken against the criminals. Governments amend laws whenever sees them as outdated. Different types of regulations that government implements may have negative impact to the school environment. The following laws can impact the school environment.

- **Changes to child protection legislation**

Governments pass laws to protect children of the country from abuse. Children face some of the following abuses:

> ➤ Use of physical punishment to discipline children
> ➤ Starving children as a form of discipline
> ➤ Negligence of parents/ guardians to take their responsibilities of supporting children

The child protection laws prevent teachers to use any form of abuse such as corporal punishment in school when trying to discipline students. If teachers fail to comply with the law and abuse students in class, parents of the children may report the incidents to the police. Consequences of teachers going to the police to answer cases of abuse interrupt classes which impacts the performance of the students.

Teachers should take necessary responsibilities to understand laws of the country so that they comprehend issues that constitute abuse and the rights of the students at school.

- ## Reducing age of starting school

Government may reduce age of starting school for example, reducing from 8 years to 6 years or from 6 years to 4 years so that children start education from preschool level so that they get prepared well before starting primary school. If the government implements such type of school policy then the number of children in school will increase. The increase of the number of students in school brings a lot of challenges such as the need to increase teachers, classroom, and special security measures for the small children, and to provide specific toilets for small children. If the school is not fully funded by the government then the implementation of the policy would be very difficult and make it impossible for parents who wish to send their children at early age.

- ## Abolishing School Leaving Age Policy

Governments may abolish school leaving age policy to encourage students to finish school. There is a tendency in most poor countries where students stop school for two years and come back. For example, student may start school in 2014 but stop in 2016 and come back in 2017 to continue with school. There are various contributing factors that cause students to delay schooling. The factors include: poverty, poor parental care, early teen age pregnancy. If the government abolishes school leaving age policy will encourage students that left school to come back to finish their school.

There are drawbacks that implicate the school environment when this policy is implemented:

> ➢ Returning students may not respect teachers as they may look older.
> ➢ Young students may learn in fear if the returning older students terrorize them
> ➢ Young students may mock returning students which may reduce their school moral
> ➢ School resources may be stretched
> ➢ Administration burden

- **Changes to opening closing hours of school**

School hours determine the time students spend at school. School teachers use hours to plan how to accomplish the syllabus of their school. The longer the hours at school the shorter the time to finish the syllabus. The shorter the hours at school the longer the time to finish the syllabus. In relation, government can decide to increase the hours spent at school by increasing the school opening hours. For example, the government can change the opening hours from 8:30 AM to 7:30 AM as and changing closing hours from 1:30 PM to 3:30 PM. In that particular situation, the government increases school hours from 5 hours to 8 Hours. The extra three hours can help the teacher to cover other subjects or lessons. However the increase of hours can bring certain repercussions, such as: psychological impact to both the students and the teachers. Teachers may feel fatigue from teaching and students may lose concentration from listening for 8 hours; teachers may demand increase of salaries; they can be strain of resources to carter the extra hours.

• Changing of school funding laws

There are many schools that are funded by charitable organizations. Other organizations are religious based organizations while others are not religious oriented organizations. The funding law that the government can pass might have a negative consequences to such organizations. For example, the government can put strict laws against funding from organizations that are regarded as terrorist organizations. Or the government can impose strict laws against funding from organizations that may be regarded as promoting immoral acts. Schools that are funded by organizations that are affected by the new law face financial difficulty. Operations of schools will be affected. The schools might close if there are no alternative financial sources.

• Health and safety legislation

Good government is the one that takes the health, safety of schools, students and teachers with high esteem. To influence health and safety, government brings legislations to protect its citizens. For better school environment the government can implement legislations that discourage building sub-standard school blocks, coming to school with guns or sharp materials, building school near a dumping site of waste, building a school along a busy high way without proper fences and fly-over bridges. New legislations of no weapon at school, for example, will enforce school management to search every student entering school premises. Such legislation empowers the teachers to deal with any student that can go against the legislation. Failing to search students may result students bringing guns to schools and kill the friends and teachers.

OTHER ENVIRONMENTS

Besides the above mentioned environments the following might have negative impacts to the school.

- **A new highway layout near the school may create new dangers for pupils**

Development is an ongoing activity in many countries. One way of developing areas is to improve road network. Government decides to build new highways after good analysis to reduce vehicle congestion on the road. The government can decide to bring new highway to carter for developments in the area. The highway can run near the school which can put students' life in danger. The school management will then be responsible to safety first. The school can erect fences and fly-over bridges in order to protect its students.

- **Reduction of green space available for activities**

The urbanization is increasing in many developing countries. The increase of urbanization leads to high demand of houses which reduces the green space available for activities like sports and others. The decrease of space available for sports, schools suffer as many students will not be able to attend sporting activities in the area.

- **Changes to local bus routes**

Most school going students relay on buses when going to school. Any disturbance of the transport will have major impact on the school. The changes to local bus routes will mean the bus that students used to take will have other routes to take. The changes will force students to walk, or find other means of transport that might be dangerous to use. It may cause students arriving late to school. The late coming of students to school will influence the outcome of results as syllabus might not be finished.

Relationship Of Teachers

CAUSES OF BAD RELATIONSHIP OF TEACHERS

The school that has poor relationship of teachers provide environment that teachers and students will not be motivated. There are many factors that cause poor relationship among teachers, factors such as lies, gossip, jealousy, hypocrisy, hatred, backbiting, etc.

LIES

Lies are practiced by people in different levels. Levels of lies can be classified into four and these are:

- Individual level lies: This is when people lie to one another and the consequence is determined to the impact of the lies to the individuals. For example, a person can lie to a friend that he/she saw his spouse with another person.
- Community level lies: This is when people lie to communities and the consequences can affect the whole community. For example, a community leader can lie to the community and advise them

to contribute to the new development that will take place in the community. But later on people realize that it was a lie.

- National level lies: This is when people lie to the nation and the consequence is determined to the impact of the lies to the nation. For example, president can lie that he/she will sell government assets to buy hospital drugs. After the selling of assets like buildings president use the money for personal use.
- World level lies: This is when people lie to the world by using different types of media to influence people to believe their lies.

REASON WHY PEOPLE LIE

- To use lies for personal gains
- To prevent the truth
- Jealousy
- Habit
- To cause harm

DANGERS OF LIES

A lie in any form is not good for the success of good relationship among teachers. Lies of many people have caused spouses to divorce, friends to fight, communities to break, wars, etc. Lying is a quality also found among teachers. Sometimes teachers lie about a colleague. A teacher who is good on lies brings confusion, hatred, fighting among fellow teachers. Allowing lies to spread at the school increases backbiting/gossip and reduces friendship. Fellow teachers should verify stories before acting on it.

People who are good in lies have skills of convincing other people. They are able to make people believe that whatever they are saying is true. For example, when you enter a shop where the owner is good in convincing people to buy a product or service by using lies, will sell the product or service which is expired and not what the customer wanted. But because the owner lied to customer, will end up buying it.

If the community finds out that a person is a liar, people don't believe what he/she will say in the future even though he/she will be talking the truth. People will believe someone who always speaks the truth.

Sources of other wars that took place in the world were based on lies. Powerful nations used powerful media to spread lies and convince people to believe that whatever they were spreading was true. Millions of people lost lives from these wars and resources of these countries were either stolen or destroyed.

JEALOUSY

Jealousy is one of the dangerous factors that bring people's success down. It is a disease found in many people. The success of a person gives other people sleepless nights. A jealousy person always tries harder to find ways how he/she can bring mischief on the success of the other person. People get jealous about leadership of person, good relationship of spouses, richness of people, and education other people. People use different ways to bring the success of other people's success down. Some of the ways people use to bring other people down are:

- Talking ill about a person: Sometimes when people are not happy about someone's success try to talk bad about the person. People try to remind his past. For example, reminding his/ her previous living standard; or reminding previous bad behavior; talking bad about things that made the person successful. Sometimes they spread false news about the successful person.
- Destroying person's property: Jealous people destroy properties of people like cars, houses, shops of the successful people. Sometimes they hire people to destroy properties on their behalf.
- Harming the successful person physically: Jealous person can even harm a successful person physically. They may even kill the successful person. Most of the time they hire people to kill the person.

It is very difficult to identify the plans of jealous person as sometimes is the same person who smile and enjoy being with you plans to destroy you.

REASONS WHY PEOPLE PRACTICE JEALOUSY

- Failing to achieve a success: Some people who fail to reach the successful level prefer to indulge in jealous in different forms.
- Monopolizing the success: Some people who have achieved success like fortunes of money and others may not like to see other people to reach the same level like them. They would like to be the only people having the success. They try to suppress any person who wants to reach the same level of success.
- Arrogance of the successful person: Some other people who have achieved success become arrogant. The arrogance causes people to feel bad about the person and plan to bring his/her success down by using ways described above.
- Habit: For other people is just a habit of jealousy. They do not like other people progressing well in life.

The level of jealousy can be classified into individual jealousy, community jealousy, and national jealousy.

- Individual jealousy: This is when a person practice jealousy to a person.

- Community jealousy: This when a community practice jealousy over a success of another community. The jealousy can come from individuals or a group of people, or the entire community against the success of the other community.
- National jealousy: This when a person, a group of people, or the entire nation practice jealousy against the success of other nations. A national jealousy is dangerous as is tantamount to come up with measures to suppress the successful nation. The jealousy country can impose restriction in trade with the successful nation, or start war to destroy the successful nation.

Whatever the reason might be, jealousy is not justifiable. The only remedy of this disease is to wish your friend what you wish for yourself. The success of your friend should be regarded as your success, and your success should be regarded as the success of the others. If people can put this little wisdom into practice there shall be prosperous in individuals, communities and nations.

HYPOCRISY

The other dangerous factor that destroys friendship of teachers is hypocrisy. It is the state of falsely claiming to posses virtuous characteristics that one lacks. People may be claiming to love a person or enjoying being with the person while in the reality he is not. The outer character is not the same with inner character. Hypocrites in societies are in abundance. In the teaching environment teachers may claim to be friends while in the reality are not and spread wrong things about colleagues.

THERE ARE THREE MAJOR SIGNS OF HYPOCRITES AND THESE ARE:

- Break promises: Hypocrites break promises which they agree with friends. They do not take promises seriously. When signing promises they only show the outer character like they agreeing with it while they are not.
- Untrustworthy: Hypocrites do not honor the trust. When people trust them with things they use them without knowledge of the owner. Hypocrites may convince people and pose themselves outwardly as honest people while they are not. When someone comes with something for them to keep they accept like they will honestly keep it while in the heart they know that they will not.
- Lies: Hypocrite use lies to deceive people. They are good in convincing people to believe what they are saying is true.

THINGS THAT HYPOCRITES LIKE TO ACHIEVE

- Personal gain
- Destroying relationship

- Corrupting people

The school that has good relationship among the teachers will have a number of benefits. There will be peace among teachers. Fighting, quarrels and gossiping will not be practiced at the school. The performance of the school will increase as many people will concentrate on the school rather than spending time on unnecessary things. There will be heart of caring and love among the teachers.

Good relationship of teachers is very important for the success of the school.

WAYS TO INCREASE GOOD RELATIONSHIP OF TEACHERS

There are many ways how good relationship among the teachers can be increased. Some of them are: social responsibility, good communication and introduction of social welfare services.

SOCIAL RESPONSIBILITY

Social responsibility can help to increase good relationship among the teachers. Social responsibility is solely aimed to help the community. Businesses and organizations introduce this responsibility to help the community. Organizations render assistance to the communities by building schools, sponsoring students, building clinics, etc. Many times staff and the management get involved physically to help the project.

Teachers can organize social responsibility activities whereby teachers can help communities. Some of the activities that teachers can introduce at school are: helping the elderly citizens with food and cleaning their houses; visiting the sick in hospitals and communities; sponsoring community sports teams; helping community orphans.

Trustees, management and the teachers of the schools can join together and physically participate on the social responsibility activities. Physical participation of every teacher can increase friendship. During social responsibility activities, people from different levels in the management do similar things regardless of the positions they hold in the hierarchy. A teacher can do similar thing with his principal. Social responsibility activities encourage teamwork, sympathy, love and positive thinking.

COMMUNICATION

The most important thing that helps good relationship among the teachers is good communication. Communication is the passing or conveying of message or an idea from one party to another in such a manner that both parties perceive its identical meaning. Effective communication helps to promote good understanding between teachers and that in return helps to reduce teachers' disputes. Too often disputes among teachers arise from simple issues that arise from poor communication.

Communication and understanding among teachers need to be taken seriously in schools. Effective communication is vital for the success of the school. Communication can either be formal or informal. Informal communication is a casual form of information sharing typically used in personal conversations with friends or family members. Formal communication refers to interchange of information officially. Informal communication is much greater to improve teachers' communication. Teachers can use oral or written communication. For example, teachers can use SMS, e-mail to communicate with fellow teachers.

WELFARE SERVICES

The school can encourage teachers and other staff members of the school to organize a welfare committee. The committee comprises with a chairman, deputy chairman, secretary general, deputy secretary and treasurer general. The committee formulates constitution that is used to guide the members of the welfare. Every member contributes monthly to ensure financial viability of the association. The welfare deals with issues such as assisting one another during time of sickness and death of members, sharing time of happiness, organizing sports activities for the staff members, promoting visiting staff members, promoting reconciliation in time of disputes, providing counseling services in a difficult time.

- Assisting members time of sickness and death

When a teacher gets sick his/ her personal power diminishes and needs support from people that are close to him/her. Any assistance that the welfare can provide to the sick person will instill a sense of belonging and love the fellow teachers/staff members have to the person. Financial support that the welfare committee can give to the affected person eases the burden of the sick person. As much is appreciated on the financial support, the moral support uplifts the spirit of the sick person. Welfare committee can send a delegation to visit the sick person either in the hospital or at home. The delegation can carry flowers and message of support from fellow employees. If the sick teacher/ staff member is very serious, the assistance can be given to his/her immediate family members like wife, husband and children.

In event of death of the member, the welfare committee can assist the bereaved family with some funeral expenses. Members of the welfare should be encouraged to attend the funeral procession of their colleague. The presence of all members will show a sincerely love members had for their friend. If the death falls on the close family member like the wife, husband or child, welfare can provide financial and moral support to the member. The assistance that welfare renders to the member will bring good relationship.

• Sharing time of happiness

Times of happiness come to every staff member. There are many occasions that people celebrate like, birthdays, weddings, anniversaries, achievements, etc. To share the moments of happiness with fellow members of the welfare strengthens the relationship. The welfare members should participate the occasion of their member and provide gifts to the welfare member. Besides the above mentioned occasions, welfare committee can organize party where all members can attend. For example, end of the year, the welfare committee can set a date where all members can be invited for the party. The welfare committee in consultation with members can chose a place where they can have the party. Members can come with their family members and enjoy the party. Meeting fellow members outside the work environment increases happiness and good relationship.

• Promoting teachers sports activities

Sports have a number of benefits that teachers can get. It is a source strengthening the body and improves health standard of the teachers. Sports can also be used as one way of promoting happiness and relationship among teachers. Welfare committee can form welfare teams where members can participate either playing or supporting. Once welfare has a well formidable team can compete in league games or tournaments. The sports activities can help to improve relationship as most members will come as people of the same family.

- **Promoting inter-teacher visiting**

Teachers must regularly visit one another in time of happiness and grief. It energizes teacher's relationship with fellow teacher.

Visiting is vital in human relationship. It seems like is a declining practice to many people including teachers and needs urgent revival. People are not the same as they were in the past. People in the past used to travel for two days or more only to go and visit friends and relatives. Traveling was difficult, walking under the scorching heat of the sun with donkeys and others by foot. In the times of happiness they used to enjoy together. In the time of sorrow they used to share their grief. This was because they used to visit one another.

Diseases we hear of and experience in this era were not unheard of. Stress was something foreign and well handled in the past. Visiting and talking to each other helped to reduce stress and other diseases. Today's people don't care about visiting one another. Yet they are better off in term of transport. People fail to visit their own parents near or far. People fail to visit their own sick relatives because of busy.

- **Promoting culture of talking and smiling**

Talking and smiling may seem like simple practices but they are beneficial to people. When people talk opens a room of communication. It reduces stress and worry. A teacher will be able to know grief or happiness of a friend when he/ she talks. Sometimes many people who commit suicide tend to be people who do not want to talk and prefer to keep their worries within themselves. Talking to fellow teachers, chatting with them and even asking about their family can encourage good relationship. It is better to get rid of the habit where other people say "I don't have time for him/her."

Smile brightens face and shows a sense of acceptance to a fellow teacher. It is not good to see teachers working together failing to talk and smile to each other.

- **Promoting reconciliation**

Reconciliation plays a big role in resolving conflicts that may erupt between teachers. Reconciliation saves lives, reputation and properties. In other circumstance only a sentence like "I am sorry please forgive me"; and the sentence like "I forgive you" can solve the entire problem. These sentences may seem simple but have saved lives, marriages and promoted love and among school teachers, communities and nations. They are simple sentences but many people find them hard to say.

For a better reconciliation a perpetrator should acknowledge his guilty and apologize. If a perpetrator fails to acknowledge that is guilty then will be hard to give any apology. But also a victim should accept apology of a perpetrator for them to be in good relationship. To have good process of reconciliation, a third person can be asked to help both parties to come up with positive results. Teachers need to resolve their misunderstandings amicably so that they will have good relationship.

Sometimes failing to reconcile between teachers may results into backbiting, jealousy, fighting, and sometimes killing of one another. It is better for teachers who notice that their fellow teachers are not in good relationship to bring them together for reconciliation.

The school teachers can understand how important reconciliation is by understanding how reconciliation was used to bring peace in many countries. Most of wars and battles fought in many countries came to an end when reconciliation was used to resolve their problems.

PROVIDING COUNSELING SERVICES

Counseling service is required to be provided at the schools to help resolving problems of teachers. Teachers face different problems from work related and family related problems. These problems bring stress to teachers which then impact to the performance in the class. Welfare committee should provide counseling services to help teachers to overcome their problems. The committee can appoint experienced matured people to help the teachers. People that are helping to handle the teacher's problems should preserve confidentiality when dealing with teacher's problems.

Qualities Of Good Students

Students are important in the education system. They are regarded as the output of the education. Although teachers have a prominent role in education, people measure the performance of the teachers by analyzing the students' performance. Teachers are regarded as the sole input of education. The success of education does not depend only on the qualities of teachers but also the qualities of students. The school can have good resources of experienced teachers, good books, good infrastructures, and good management but if the students lack good qualities, the dissemination of education will be difficult. For example, the soccer team might have a best coach, facilities, and best financial rewards but if players are of poor quality the team will struggle. The following are some of the qualities that enable students to succeed:

LISTENING

A quality of listening is essential for the success of the students. Good students that posses this quality produce good results. There are two areas where students fail to grasp the lesson, the willingness to listen and the ability to listen.

• **Willingness to listen**

The stumbling block in education is the unwillingness of students to listen from the teachers. In class, students should have willingness to listen to their teachers if they want education. How do you feel when someone you are talking to is not paying attention? You feel bad, embarrassed and sometimes you may just stop talking. It is the same in class where a teacher is teaching a lesson but only 30% of the class is paying attention, the rest of the class is not. The teachers feel frustrated because they feel that their effort is wasted.

Students divert their attention from the teachers by playing with cell phones in class and make noise that causes distractions. The lesson that should have taken one hour to finish will take two days or more to finish because of unwillingness of students. A good student always pay attention to teachers, accepts what they want from him/her to do, for example writing tests, answer questions, reading, etc.

• **Ability to listen -Listening skills**

Active listening is a skill that can be acquired and developed with good practice. Active listening means fully concentrating on what is being said rather than just passively hearing the message of the teacher. Active listening involves listening with all senses as well as giving full attention to the teacher. It is important that the active listener (student) is also seen to be listening otherwise the teacher may conclude that what he/she is talking about is uninteresting to the students. Interest can be conveyed to the teacher by using both verbal and non-verbal messages such as maintaining eye contact, nodding head and smiling, agreeing by saying 'yes'.

Feedback is important in the listening process. By providing feedback the person speaking will usually feel more at ease and therefore communicate easily, openly and honestly. Listening is the most fundamental component of interpersonal communication skills. Listening is an active process in which a conscious decision is made to listen and understand the message of the speaker. Active listening is also about patience. Pauses and short periods of silence should be accepted. Students should not be tempted to jump in with questions or comments every time there are few seconds of silence. Listening is the ability to accurately receive and interpret messages in communication process. Students can ask for clarification when they cannot make sense of the teacher. Sometimes, the messages that the teacher is attempting to send can be complex, involving many different people, issues, places and times. Through clarification it is possible for the teacher and students to make sense of confusions and complex issues.

ABILITY TO FORM A STUDY TIME TABLE

Study time table plays a vital role for the education of students. It is a plan that a student can use to study the lessons of school. Before designing the time table the students should identify a number of factors that could implicate the success of the time table. The students should know the number of subjects they are taking, the contents of the subjects, the time frame that can be used for studying subjects before examination, the place of study, and the time each subject can take to study.

The sequence of the subjects is also a considerable factor. For example, after studying the solving subject like Mathematics the students should avoid following it with another solving subject or scientific subject. Mathematics should be followed with language, or theory subjects like History, Business Studies, and Economics, etc.

The students can allocate 2 hours for the solving subjects and 1hour 30 minutes for the solving subjects. The students should prefer quiet time during the morning or the night to study. During the day the students can use their free time to study at quite places. The students should avoid communicating friends using phones while studying.

STUDY TIME TABLE FOR HIGH SCHOOL STUDENT

DAY	AM HOURS		PM HOURS	
Monday			Mathematics	English
Tuesday	SCHOOL TIME		Statistics	Business studies
Wednesday			Accounting	Economics
Thursday			Mathematics	English
Friday			Statistics	Business studies
Saturday	Accounting	Economics	Business studies	Mathematics
Sunday	Statistics	English	Mathematics	Economics

RESPECTING TEACHERS

Teachers play an important role in the lives of students. Besides the parents they also shape lives of students by imparting knowledge and help to inculcate good morals in the students' life. They act as agent of change and do advise students in their choice of careers. Teachers can really influence the lives of many students, especially when they act as good role model. Many students are able to remember teachers who in one way or the other influenced their lives.

Indeed, teachers can sharpen the failure and success of the students. They can help dull students to become brilliant. It is, therefore, necessary for students to develop good relationship with teachers by listening them at all times.

However, despite the meaningful role of teachers in lives of students, some throw paroxysms, curse, insult or even attack teachers. They forget that teachers, whether young or old, complement the role of their parents, therefore, they need to give them their due respect.

Students give teachers all sorts of names, and refuse to give them the respect that they deserve. The students should remember that a teacher, like a parent, punishes not out of hatred but love. When students are well disciplined, recognition goes to the teachers as well as the school. Students should not see teachers as enemies.

Students should show teachers respect in words or actions. For example to be quite in class, positively responding to the needs of the teachers, helping the teachers to carry their bags and other materials, asking permission when going out of the class. Students should speak words like: thank you sir/madam, please sir/madam, and all other words of respect.

One student said, "My teachers deserve all my respect. No matter how better educations I can get but when I meet them they deserve my respect. My respect goes first to my teacher who taught me alphabet and then all teachers who educated me. I feel like to getting heart attack when I hear that students hit or shoot teachers. This is like hitting and killing your own parents. The teacher takes time to think of ways how to help the students. It is a curse when a student mock, hit or kill his own teacher. A student's teacher will remain his/her teacher even though the student can get better education than the teacher.

Respecting is the behavior that should be practiced by teachers and students. It is not a behavior that is accomplished by only a certain group of people. For example, respect cannot only be practiced by the employees over their employers, or the poor towards the rich, the illiterate towards the educated, the child towards the elders, and the subordinates towards the leaders.

Other people view respect as a practice of the disadvantaged group over the advantaged group. For example: A maid worked as a domestic worker for over 20 years. She grew up working as a domestic worker. She nursed most of employer's children until they become men and women. Over the years the employer and his children insulted the maid. Shouted her on useless things and called her bad names like monkey and donkey. The maid continued respecting the employer even the boss's children whom she changed their napkins and bathing them, called them bosses, sir, Mr., madam, as words of respect. But the employer and his children failed to respect her even to recognize her motherly role she played.

The rich people should also show initiative to respect the poor as it is advisable for the teachers to respect the students so that students will be able to respect their teachers. The teacher can gain respect from the students from various ways. Some of them are:

- Respecting the students: The teachers should not be rude when talking to the students. The teacher should know every student's story and treat each as an individual.

- Be part of the learning community: The teacher should not be the boss of learning. Encourage students to take ownership of their learning.
- Acknowledge students' physical needs: Allow students to drink water, go to toilet, and eat when it is necessary.
- Be fair and reasonable: The teacher should not be bias when teaching students
- Provide a secure learning space: The teacher should provide a safe and secure environment for his/her students
- Provide rules: The teacher should set out rules of the class and provide a distinction between the teacher and students
- Be sincere: The teacher should be honest and trustworthy
- Self respect: The teacher should respect himself/herself by knowing what to talk and do with students
- Look smart: Looking smart provide honor and respect from the students

RESPECTING PARENTS

When some students start job, get rich and busy with accumulating of wealth forget the role parents played in the student's life. They abuse parents by kicking them, even killing them. Others take their parents and dump them at the old age home without valid reason. Instead for the students to use the fortunes of wealthy they accumulate by looking after the parents in their houses.

The respect of the parents is diminishing every day. Many children don't know how to talk to their parents; they don't know how to respond to them. But the mother is the one who kept the student for nine months or above in her stomach, gave birth to him/her, cared him/her during time of hardship above hardship. The parents took time of feeding, bathing and supporting the child who then becomes successful in life.

POEM - A CRY OF AN OLD LADY

IF TO HAVE A CHILD IS TO BE KICKED

THEN THAT CHILD IS NOT MINE

IF TO HAVE A CHILD IS TO BE DUMPED IN OLD
AGE HOMES

THEN THAT CHILD IS NOT MINE

IF TO HAVE A CHILD IS TO BE KILLED

THEN THAT CHILD IS NOT MINE

IF TO HAVE A CHILD IS TO BE DRIVEN OUT OF
MY HOUSE

THEN THAT CHILD IS NOT MINE

IF TO HAVE A CHILD IS TO VISIT HIM IN PRISON

EVERY TIME

THEN THAT CHILD IS NOT MINE

IF TO HAVE A CHILD IS TO BE EMBARRASSED

THEN THAT CHILD IS NOT MINE

I ALLOWED TO KEEP HIM IN MY STOMACH

BUT TODAY IS DUMPING ME

I SACRIFICED MY BACK TO CARRY HIM

BUT TODAY IS DUMPING ME

I SACRIFICED MY TIME TO FEED HIM

BUT TODAY IS DUMPING ME

I SLEPT SLEEPLESS NIGHTS FOR HIM

BUT TODAY IS DUMPING ME

I SPENT ALL MY MONEY FOR HIM

BUT TODAY IS DUMPING ME

IF TO HAVE THAT CHILD WAS A CHOICE

NO ONE WOULD HAVE CHOSEN HIM

By Manaf Katonga

HARD WORKING

Apathy is the disease of many students today. Most of them are not prepared to face problems. They want to get things without effort. Students should consider the effort that the baby puts before starts walking. The baby falls many times before he/she knows how to stand, walk, and run. The baby doesn't lose hope. With determination she/he keeps trying until she/he knows how to walk.

Students should not go to school because parents force them to go to school. They should go to school because they want to learn. When students go to school on their own willingness will work hard. The students should go extra mile to get education by joining additional classes, participating in reading groups, spending time in libraries, and others. A hardworking student will make teachers tired by asking questions and requesting clarifications in lessons.

"I worked hard for this" are always words coming from the father after seeing that his children are not taking care of things he provides them. They are words calling for attention. Many people have seen friends improving in life after facing a lot of problems. They worked hard and achieved what they desired like business, education and jobs. Nothing comes easy in life. In every person's life there are times of difficult and happiness. A person should keep on trying until he/she achieves what he/she wants. Knock until the door is open!

FACTORS THAT DERAIL HARD WORKING OF STUDENTS

- **Apathy**

In every school, while there are hardworking students, there are also lazy students who are not interested in anything about school. They just come to school, sit at the back of the class, talk and disturb others.

- **Poor family interest on students' education**

The most common factor which influences the academic performance of students is the family. If the parents are interested on the work of their children at school, the students will be more interested in their lessons too. Educated parents generally show more interest in the academic performance of the students. When parents are not interested in the success or failure of their children, the children will not be serious with school and eventually will poorly perform in examination.

- **Poverty**

The other factor that influences the lack of interest of students on education is the poor financial position of the family. There are brilliant poor students who are capable to study in universities but fail to enroll university studies because they are poor. Some students are forced to work after school to get money to pay school fees, transport and buy stationeries for school; as a result, they fail to concentrate on school work.

• **Dream -busters**

Dream-busters also implicate education of the students. Dream-busters are those people who always de-motivate others by coming up with negative thinking about the success of the person. Many people have failed to succeed in life because of following the dream busters. The students should avoid such kind of people, who might come with smiling faces while they do not want them achieve education.

• **Peer pressure**

A human needs a friend for support, help and advice. If the person does not have friends many things become difficult. Sometimes friends play a bigger role in a person's life than his own relatives. Friends can help to solve things which can be difficult for a family member to solve. The important element in choosing a friend is the type of friend students should have to continue with education.

The problem faced by many students is the choice of good friend. Other students prefer to have friends who have bad behavior like drinking alcohol, smoking drugs, gambling. Other students manage to choose good friends that are school lovers. The former type of friends drive students to bad behavior and will eventually lose interest in school while the later type of friends drive students to good behavior and will eventually work hard in school.

Peer pressure encourages students to change their attitudes, values, or behaviors to conform the group's norm. Peers become an important influence on behavior during adolescent stage, and peer pressure has been called a hallmark of an adolescent level experience. Peer pressure drives many students to wrong direction. A student may be involved in stealing, smoking, robbery, killing of people because of bad friends.

Parents and friends start noticing the changing behavior of the student once they see that the good behavior of the student is diminishing. Parents and friends notice explicit behavior like, coming home of the student under the influence of alcohol, talking rude and poor school performance.

Peer pressure is not all bad. It can also have a positive impact to a behavior of a student. There are many people who changed their behavior to good behavior when their friends convinced them. Former gangsters, gamblers, thieves, murderers, changed their behavior too be good and became leaders and role model of the people. Most of them changed bad behavior because of good peer pressure.

FACTORS THAT INFLUENCE HARDWORKING OF STUDENTS

There are various factors that can influence students in school's performance. Parents have a very strong influence that can affect students' performance. Students must learn to devote their time and effort and exercise diligence and patience while studying. Besides parents the following are other factors that influence hardworking of students.

- **Punctuality**

Punctuality is an important part of self discipline and is essential to hardworking. Students should make sure that they are in class at the right time. Late coming to class signifies laziness of students towards school. They come late to school and increase absenteeism without valid reasons. For any minor sickness will be an excuse for them to stay at home time of learning school. Punctual students will not find it hard when they start working in a company. They will be able to attend meetings, appointments, and work commitments at the right time.

- **Group work of students**

Students can also learn well when they are actively involved in school work by using formal learning groups and study teams. Teachers can encourage groups to do certain educational using formal learning groups. Formal learning groups are teams established to complete a specific task, such as, writing a report, performing lab experiment, and carry out projects. These groups may complete their work in a single class session or over several weeks. Typically, students work together until the task is finished, and their project is graded.

Study teams are long-term groups with stable membership whose primary responsibility is to provide members with support, encouragement, and assistance in completing course requirements and assignments. Study teams also inform their members about lectures and assignments when someone has missed a session. The larger the class and the more complex the subject matter, the more valuable study teams can be. Students work hard so that their group should successfully achieve the task.

Many students have never worked in collaborative learning groups and may need practice in such skills as active and tolerant listening, helping one another in mastering contents, giving and receiving constructive criticism, and managing disagreements. Teachers should discuss these skills with students and reinforce them during classes. The students in a team must perceive that they sink or swim together, that each member is responsible to and dependent on all the others, and that team cannot succeed unless all in the team succeed. Knowing that peer is relying on you is a powerful motivator for group work.

Group work helps students to work with others that they might fear to talk to or feel shy to play with because of differences of financial status, color, tribe and/or nationality. If the student has a direct contact with others he/she will be able to deal with different people despite their background. The students that grow working with different people will find it easy to have friends.

When students work in groups learn also on how they can be followers. The work group can reduce the problem of leadership battle which is largely growing. Many people want to be leaders; no one is prepared to be a follower. Others do that because they don't want a certain person to be a leader because of the color, religion, selfishness, discrimination, etc. But students who have dealt with different students in different groups will accept the leader despite differences in their background.

Although people debate whether leaders are made or born, the point is, we are all leaders and we are all followers, the difference is the level, type, situation of leadership one posses. A President can be a follower in the mosque or in the church and leaders in the mosques or churches can be followers in companies, communities, countries, etc.

The student is a follower to his parents but he/she can be a leader in school and can be a follower to his captain in the sports ground. What is most important is the ability of the student to adapt to be a leader in one situation and to be a follower in another situation.

• **Punishment of students**

Punishment is aimed at disciplining the students from the bad actions they do and to give other students a lesson so that they should not repeat the same problem. Law and order is highly preserved if punishment is observed at school.

Punishment is also practiced at work, in the family, in the community. Many laws and orders are passed when people continue having unacceptable behavior. The schools that do not have laws face difficulty when deciding to punish students because students cannot be punished if there are no laws to follow at the schools.

Law is the uniform of which every student is required to follow. Laws should not favor certain group of students. Punishment should not be biased for or biased against certain group of students. Whether the student is big or small, poor or rich, if found guilty the law should take its cause and used equally.

Unfortunately punishment is enforced against the vulnerable people like the poor students just like the way punishment is used in different countries, for example, many prisons in different countries are full of the weak and poor people who cannot defend themselves. For example, a man who stole a small bottle of Coca-Cola soft drink saved over 8 months jail term while the other person who robbed millions in the company spent few days in prison.

The teacher giving the punishment should be the justice person. Impartiality must be a code of practice by that teacher. If there are two students accusing each other, both of them should be given equal chance to explain their side of the story. The teacher should not judge one-sided story. All witnesses should be given a reasonable chance to explain their sides.

The punishment given should be equivalent to the rule that the student break. It will not be regarded as justice if the teacher gives harsh punishment to students when the rule broke requires simple punishment. There will be no justice to give punishment to students who are innocent.

OTHER CHALLENGES OF EDUCATION

In addition to what mentioned above the following are the other challenges in education.

DROP-OUTS FROM SCHOOLS

There are many countries where students are dedicated to obtain good education. This is contrary to other countries where school education is taken for granted. Parents don't bother to send their children to school. The problem is serious to girls. The parents force girls to abandon school and marry them to men at a small age because of poverty. Students are not able to get stationeries, uniforms, and pay school fees because of poverty. Students that are brilliant in class end up to be unskilled labors as they drop out schools because of poverty. The poor families continue to have bad jobs while the rich families continue to have generation of graduates and become bosses in companies.

Other students drop out from school because of the level of education offered at the school. In the rural areas in many poor countries high schools and colleges are scarce. Once the students finish the primary level they fail to pursue education because of the scarcity of high schools and colleges. People who have relatives in town send their children to further their education.

The school resources can be another factor that discourages students from continuing school. If the school does not have enough resources like books and teachers might force other students to drop school.

STUDENTS' DRUG ABUSE

Dealing in drugs is rising in developed and developing countries. The drug dealers form part of the communities. Others are known to the community while others are not. Other drug dealers become leaders of the communities and people respect them because of the money they get from drug dealings. Some of the drug dealers contribute to some of the social welfare organizations. They give food to the poor people from the dirty money they accumulate. But people know that drug abuse is killing students and destroys families. The communities are getting worse day by day because of drug abuse.

IMPACTS OF DRUG ABUSE

- Many students come with the influence of drugs to school. They disturb classes and sometimes cause injuries and death to teachers and fellow students. Violence is increasing in many schools. The number of students killed by fellow schoolmates is increasing. The playing grounds are no longer safe grounds in many schools. They become fighting and smoking grounds. The environment in many schools enhances fear in the hearts of many students when coming to school.

- Drop out of school has increased in many schools where influence of drugs is rampant. Most of the drug addicted students take control of classes. Their behavior may enforce other students to leave school out of fear from the drug addicted students. The drop outs increases also when drug addicted students consider school as not important in their lives and prefer to leave school.

- There is increase of theft and robbery. Students even steal money or sell school and parents' assets for drugs. It is common to hear that drug addicted students steal TVs, laptops of their parents and friends and sell them to get money to buy drugs. In many instances they sell the assets at cheap price. Sometimes these drug addicted students break houses and rob people in the streets so that they get money to buy drugs. The consequences of theft and robbery are injury, jail or death. There is an increase of jail inmates because of the increase of drug abuse and related substances. Many students have died because of their involvement in theft and robbery.

- There is psychological impact to the students in families when parents are involved in the drug abuse. Students live with hunger for many days yet the parents are working. Students fail to get money to buy food, pay school fees, buy stationeries and their enthusiasms for school diminish and then decide to leave school. When parents continue abusing drugs end up losing businesses, jobs and properties. Their children eventually end up failing to continue with school.

POEM - I WALK IN THE STREET OF DRUGS

I WALK IN THE STREET OF DRUGS

DRAGGING ME TO THE WORLD OF NO WHERE

TAKING ME OUT FROM THE LIFE OF HAPPINESS

SENDING ME TO THE FIRE OF HELL

HAD IT BEEN THE DRUG IS A GIFT

I WOULD HAVE GIVEN IT BACK TO HIM

I 'M HOLDING A LIFE OF MISERY AND FAILURE

FAILING TO SEE WHAT IS MY FUTURE

WALKING LIKE SHEEP WITH NO SHEPHERD

WHERE IS MY FAMILY

WHERE IS MY BUSINESS

DRUGS HAVE TAKEN AWAY

I WALK IN THE STREET OF DRUGS

By Manaf Katonga

WAYS TO REDUCE DRUG ABUSE

- Government regulations. The government should provide tough laws to any person involved in drugs either selling or smoking. It is the government regulations, policing and good courts that can prevent the huge inflow and abuse of drugs in the country. There are other countries that are very lenient when dealing with drug abuse and the consequence is that the drug abuse is rising and causing huge social problems and governments find it difficult to control them.

- Strict rules in school. The school should formulate rules that prevent the use of drugs in school. The school can formulate rules that if any student is found with the influence of drugs or is known from the community about his habit of drug abuse shall be expelled from school/ or shall be prevented to register at the school. It is imperative that the head teacher/principal put necessary measures to ensure that the rules are respected and followed.

- Choosing good friends. Students should be advised to choose good friends. Because a student may change because of the influence of friends. If student's friends take drugs, he/she shall one day test and join the gang of smoking drugs. If the teacher discovers that the good student is involved with wrong friends, he/she should take initiative of advising and forcing the student out of the bad students. The teacher should involve the parents if there is a need to do so.

- Watching good movies. The movies that students watch need to be supervised very well. Major part of the behavior changes of students is coming from the movies they watch. If the students watch movies wherein drug abuse is practiced, students are attempted and regard it as the habit that successful people do. Other students became pornography lovers because of the porn movies and others became rude because of watching rude movies. Teachers should investigate type of movies that students watch.

- Regular drug talks. The school can have regular talks on drugs. The school can invite former drug abuser who can help to make students understand the dangers of using drugs. The school can show the students movies that discourage the use of drugs.

YOUTH AGE

Youth is best understood as a period of transition from dependence of childhood to adulthood's independence. Youth age is the stage that determines people's future. Other people are good today because they used their youth age to the best while others are suffering because of their failure to use their youth age to the best. It is this age that old people would wish to come back to rectify their mistakes. There are many people that feel that their youth age was spent on drugs, playing, stealing, etc. They failed to go to school to acquire education. When you see someone playing with youth age, just know that the person will cry in future.

The teacher should encourage students to work hard in school while they are still young. And that they should repeal the notion that they will be with parents forever. Youths are the pillars of the nation. The youths can change things to the better. In the year 2011, the world experienced youths changing political landscape in the Arab countries like Tunisia, Libya and Egypt. However students are not advised to change things by the use of violence such as burning schools, hospitals, libraries, etc. The tendency of using violence by young people will determine the future of the kinds of adults that are going to be in the future.

The youths of today have many opportunities which were not available in the time of their parents. Nowadays, they are many infrastructures than before where youths can use them for their benefits. Addition to that support services from the government, NGO's, communities are many. There are scholarship programs, sports facilities, counseling centers, learner-ship programs and many more. But many youths don't want to take advantage of aforementioned programs and facilities. The teacher should advise the students that their parents want them to learn school so that they become good role models for others.

A child might be coming from a rich family and possess all the required resources of life but fail to take education seriously. But when the wealth gets finish is when he/she might wish to take education seriously which most of the time does not work. The richness and poverty of the family should not derail the ability of the child to go to school. A student must be able to adapt to situation properly for the better future. If he/she is rich or poor must know how to deal with the situation properly. A story below gives a good picture on why students should value their youth age.

A man told his son a story of a certain person who had gold but did not know that it was gold and that was a precious mineral. One day he went to town carrying it. While in town he started playing with it in the street. A man coming from the opposite direction told him that he was playing with a precious mineral and he should keep it safe. The boy did not take advice of the man. Later on thieves came to hit and stole his gold. They sold it for a huge amount of money. The boy lost the gold and he was injured. The father interpreted the story to the son by telling him that gold in the story resembles the youth age. If any youthful person does not care of his/her youth age and fail to use it in the proper way he/she will lose a lot of things in life.

The teacher should advise the students that the youth age if used properly can produce good leaders in the world. Today's world leaders are there after passing a youth age like anyone else. But because they worked hard in school they became leaders in different positions. Others are presidents, ministers, board chairmen, etc. The young people to become good leaders should not only work hard in school but also working hard in the good behavior. The bad behaving leaders would mean that they grew up with bad behavior.

Students who do not listen to parents and teachers become bad leaders. Their leadership does not value human values. They get interested of enrichment by the use of fraud, oppression while people starve with hunger. When the time of election comes they fight to be leaders, but when they are elected they forget their duty of looking after their people. Good leaders feel bad when they see people suffer.

Teachers should advise students to stop spending time drinking beer and taking drugs because they are sources of bad habits and behaviors. Students start drinking beer because of peer pressure. A lot of students think that they will leave the bad behavior when they grow up and become men. In most cases it does not happen as for many it becomes a way of life. Consequently they become leaders and hold high positions in the societies and nations. Some people lose jobs because of the habit of drinking alcohol.

ROLE OF PARENTS IN EDUCATING CHILDREN

Parents have various roles to play in education of the students. Below are some roles parents should play in education of the students. They may include looking after children, relationship with school and inter-parental relationship.

LOOKING AFTER CHILDREN

It is the duty of both parents to see that their children are growing physically, spiritually and intellectually well. It is the primary duty of the parents to feed, cloth, protect and advise children so that they become good students. There are many situations where students fail to further education because parents fail to look after them in areas of food and clothes. Astonishing enough is to see parents that are able to buy food and clothes of their children fail to do so because of lack of interest.

Other students fail to continue / or are expelled from school because of a failure of parents from advising the students to behave well. Many parents have transferred parental care to teachers. Although teachers are regarded as parents of students at school, they cannot take all parental responsibilities. Limited time and number of students cannot make them good parents. It is the responsibility of the parents to supervise their children so that will be able to know their friends and advise them where necessary.

The absence of parents because of work related issues has increased the impact of students' behavior. Parents must preach what they practice. Children learn quickly by seeing what parents do. If parents advise their children something contrary to what they do, children don't take it seriously.

PARENTS - SCHOOL RELATIONSHIP

There should be a two-way communication between teachers and parents. A teacher must inform parents what their child is doing at school. A teacher can do so by calling parents and have a meeting with them, or sending letters to them. Parents should have interest in their child's work. If the child does not bring any homework, it is the responsibility of the parents to enquire by checking the books of the child or asking his/her friends because they are some children who don't like to do school work.

Parent must support teachers. They should educate the children to respect teachers. It is not advisable for parents to defend their children when they do wrong things at school. Parents that defend their children when they are wrong encourage them to disrespect teachers at school.

The parents should be careful with different allegations their children bring home from school. Some children come home with different allegations such as "my teacher hit me without reason; the teacher wanted to rape me; the school is collecting money for excursion." If parents hasten to take action without finding out from the school, may harm teachers or lose money. Children have many tactics to harm teachers or to get money from their parents. If they want to go out with their friends they might come with different allegations to their parents.

When children come home with the claim that they have been abused by the teacher, many parents run to the school and start fighting with the teacher while others insult the teacher before getting the truth from the teacher. Many parents believe whatever their child tells them is true and the teacher is a liar. Other parents take wrong decision by stopping their children from going to school without the proper proof of what transpired. The teacher should be wise enough in handling matters for a better relationship with parents.

PARENTS' RELATIONSHIP

Parents' confrontations may arise in communities because of school to large extent that parents fight. Some parents don't like to see children of other parents doing better than their children. They want their children to have good marks even if they poorly perform in school. If their friend's children improve and beat their children, the parents start making accusations against the teacher that he/she has been bribed by the other parents. Parents from the same community start breaking relationship because of the good performance of the other children. Instead of going to the teacher and find out why their children performed badly and how the teacher can help to improve the performance of their children, they prefer to keep quiet and start gossiping.

Although these parents break their relationship, you will find that the children's relationship is maintained. They play together and they don't care what is going on with the relationship of their parents. Parents should cooperate for the success of their children.

COMMUNITY

A successful community is a community that is united. A united community is formed from united families. When families are not united the communities fall apart. Families must be united so that they can defend their communities from indulging into matters which will tear the communities apart like drugs, alcohol, divorce, etc. Communities that allowed drug abuse, alcohol and divorce have failed to move forward. They are communities that have no good future and hopes.

There are many communities where people used to walk without fear, people were God-fearing, neighbors loved and supported one another, and families continuously visited one another and lived for years without quarrels and divorce. Today, these communities have turned into bad communities where people fail to walk in the night; people are self centered, gossiping is high, Jealousy is the daily life, neighbors hate one another, relatives fight in courts for small pertinent problems. All these because of the problems mentioned above and poor community leaders.

There is no community leadership in many communities. Leadership is left in the hands of selfish people who are not prepared to take problems of the community as their first priority. But communities want leaders that are there to uplift the standards of the communities. People want to see their communities progressing well, seeing children doing well in their lives, families coming together and supporting each other. The community leadership should be responsible to deal with all activities of the community like, spiritual activities, education, conflict solution, and supporting services to the elderly, widows, orphans, and many more. With good community leadership, the community can build schools, clinics, mosques, churches, sports facilities and become successful community.

COMMUNITY COMMITTEE MEMBERS

Committee members are members chosen or selected to cater for the needs of the community at large. They represent the members to oversee that the community's ideology and ideas are carried in a way that pleases the community. A committee follows the policy of the community. A committee is responsible to bring people together so that community members avoid the practice of individualism.

When selecting committee members, people must choose people who have interest of uplifting the community for the benefit of all members. The number of committee members will be determined according to the duties to be carried out and according to the number of community members. There will be no use to have big committee while the duties and number of community members is less. They should be committee members who are honest in their dealings. Members who have bad character and behavior should not represent people in the committee. If people choose corrupt leaders will bring the community down.

The committee should have a chairman, secretary, and treasurer. It can also have departments that committee and community members decide such as, education, social, security, etc. The committee has to set up executive and community meetings to keep the flow of information and to resolve issues. Some of the responsibilities of the committee are: The committee is responsible to inform the community about financial standings of the committee. The committee is also responsible to ensure that the committee operates in accordance with legal and the statutory requirements of the country concerned.

The committee is the leadership of the community. The committee has to accept full responsibilities of the community; the dealings must be honest, fair and just. Its actions and decisions on all matters relating to community must be impartial and well-balanced. It has to show consistency in actions. In addition, the leadership must display interest to the community. The committee must have cordial relations, maintain politeness, courteous and friendly relations with members of the community and be a role model to the community. In communities where there is school, teachers need to be supported, respected and protected. The committee should make teachers feel part of the community.

If there is a community school which was built by community, all day-to-day running of school should be left in the hands of the school management. Management of the school should include the principal, administrators, supervisors who are employed to run the school in a perfect way. The management report to the committee and government authorities.

Management involves ensuring that a group of people work together in the most effective and efficient manner to achieve a stated goal. Management will have to deal with planning, organizing, co- coordinating, motivating and controlling.

Planning entails how the pre-determined objectives of the school should be achieved in the most efficient way in accordance with the policy. Organizing involves putting the plans into practice, so arranging the work to be performed that the objectives will be achieved. Co-coordinating involves ensuring that although the different staff might perform different work all their efforts mesh smoothly together and are directed towards achieving the objectives. Motivating involves inspiring the staff so that they can give their best. Controlling involves supervising the people employed, checking their work and the materials they use for their work.

Recruitment of teachers can either be from the community or outside the community. Internal recruitment will give teachers in the community chance to help their own community. It will be easy for them to get used with things surrounding them as they live and grow there. Care should be taken because some other people when recruited from within the community don't take the job seriously. Recruitment should only be upon those people interested to help the community. Care also should be taken with internal recruitment to avoid any resentment and jealousy from other community members.

Before a particular vacancy is filled, applicant specification is important which entails work the successful applicant will be required to perform and what attributes in terms of skills, technical knowledge, and previous working experience, personal qualities will be required to execute the task well. Job description will then be made from the information obtained from job analysis. It contains job title, brief statement of the purpose of the job, a list of all the tasks and duties involved in the job, details of the responsibility of the post holder, that is for what he/she will be responsible, facts about the environment, details of such matters as hours of work, overtime, holidays, sick leave, etc. Full details of salary or wage rate, overtime rates, bonuses etc. Many people employ people without telling them their job description. A worker should not start working without knowing the job description.

Prospective applicants will apply either by writing a letter or by filling the forms. The person who will fulfill the requirements will be invited for an interview. The aim of the interview is to enable the interviewer to confirm the information already provided by the candidate, to obtain more information, to read original documents, to enable a candidate to obtain more information about the school and the terms and conditions of employment. The successful candidate will then be selected to start the job at a trial period (probation). It can be up to three months. This period allows the employer to determine whether the new employee can perform the work required of him or can be trained to perform. It also allows the new employee time in which to decide whether he will be happy working for the employer.

Training and education is good for the new employees. That might involve the establishment of specific training schemes. For the teacher there will be some new things established which will require some training and education. A person can be highly qualified but do not know to operate certain machine that is used for the task employed for. Some training and education will be needed for him/her.

REMUNERATION OF TEACHERS

Teachers are less paid people in many places. They can work for many years and price of commodities can rise four times but their salaries remain the same. Some people regard teachers as people who work for few hours. However the work of the teacher starts from home and end at home. Teachers spend hour at home in the morning/night preparing lessons. After lesson teachers also spend hours and sometimes use weekends marking test, homework and examinations of students. They are doing a great job for the communities. Teaching a person is not an easy task. But people only think of the time a teacher spends in classes.

DISCIPLINARY ACTION

If the teacher comes early in the morning intending to work as usual, but when he reaches there he finds that his service has been terminated, no reason is given and he/she is not given a chance to answer the case alleged, is regarded as unfair dismissal.

When the teacher is found guilty, he/she must appear by the disciplinary committee and should be allowed to explain his/her side of the story. Sometimes teacher's colleagues can come with false stories so that the fellow teacher should be dismissed from work. If the employer listens one side of the story will oppress the defendant as he/she might be a victim. When he/she if found guilty, a warning should be issued depending to the type of offence. If it is a gross misconduct the job can be terminated. Care should taken when following rules and regulations of the country as what might be termed gross misconduct in one country is not gross misconduct in another country. Some of the things that might cause the teacher facing the disciplinary committee are: failing to teach, abusing children, abusing school materials, fighting with other teachers, creating problems, etc.

The person dismissed might have good relations with the rest of the people in the working place. It is possible that his absence will influence others. Some would wish to resign. Some students might wish to leave school and other workers might wish to go on strike. Some will be grieved. Care should be taken to make sure that the departure of the person will not disrupt service rendered. Measures should be put in place to counsel the concerned people to avoid disaster at work.

RESIGNATION OF TEACHERS

In certain circumstances employer/management may try to keep the experienced teacher but the teacher may wish to resign. When resignation is voluntary and amicable, and the required "period of notice" to leave has been given, it is well worth while the employer having an "exit interview" with the teacher concerned to try and ascertain the real reason why he or she is leaving. In many cases resignations are unavoidable due to certain circumstances, for instance illness, poor health, an accident, marriage, spouse works in different town or area; pregnancy and the woman does not intend to return to work; an intended move by the teacher to another town, country; transport difficulties in getting to and from work, etc.

The employer can generally do little or nothing in such cases, but other reasons for resignations might be pause for thought. After all, if there is something wrong in the organization or business with its policies, it should be investigated and steps taken to rectify it if possible.

What can be called "avoidable" resignations generally concern terms and conditions of work, particularly salary or wages paid; dislike of physical working conditions or lack of job satisfaction. In some cases and if resources are adequate management should take measures to keep good teachers if they leave because of avoidable reasons listed above. Of course, departing teacher might not necessarily give the true reasons for leaving, but exit interviews might throw some light on it.

Some resignations are tendered in the heat of the moment and might well be withdrawn after "cooling off" period and a counseling session with the employer. Other resignations might be made to gain attention. Such resignations are not really intended to be "accepted" and so the resignation of the teacher concerned must be handled gently and carefully to ascertain the root of the problem, and then an attempt made to find a solution.

Whenever possible, the departure of a teacher should be handled amicably and with goodwill on both sides. It could be that it frequently happens that an employee is unhappy with the new job, and wants to return to his former organization. If a teacher would be welcomed back, then the employer must make this fact (tactfully) known; some people might be embarrassed to ask for the job back or nervous about being rejected or unwelcome.

The stability of teachers is necessary. Some employers don't bother when their employees leave. They have a tendency of saying "You can go I will get someone tomorrow". If there will be that friction or disagreement, some former employees might plan to come and rob the organization/school because of the failure of the employer to address their problems properly. The organization/school will create a lot of enemies.

COMMUNICATION

Effective communication is important to maintain good school relations. Vertical communication is a communication between the senior and the subordinates. It must operate in both directions: upwards as well as downwards. It is important for teachers to be able to make known quickly to those of their seniors/principals concerned any complaints or grievances they might have - and, of course to have faith that attention will be paid to them and that action will be taken quickly. In this way minor grievances will not grow into major ones because of resentment about management's apparent lack of interest. Seniors must tell their subordinates what they want other than keeping it for themselves. Vertical communication will also involve flow of instructions and solving of problems from the seniors.

Horizontal communication is a sideways or lateral-communication within the organization. This will be the flow of information between personnel of about equivalent status in different departments. Horizontal communication is concerned with the flow of information and not the flow of instructions or authority. Horizontal communication can only be effective if there is co-operation between the various departments. Seniors must encourage a spirit of co-operation and co-ordination to avoid loss of efficiency in the organization as a whole.

But despite the common interest of departments in achieving the common goal, difficulties can arise which seniors might be unaware. If not checked, personalities and personal relationships can bedevil horizontal communication. For example, if there are personality clashes, jealousies, or other causes of friction between departments (and even section) leaders, co-operation might be minimal and there might be a reluctance, or worse, to pass on information. What is called "empire building" - the attempt by a departmental leader to increase his department's (and, in consequence, his own) importance or influence- can also be a problem, as there might be reluctance to pass on information, which might "help" another department.

External communication is a communication with people or organizations outside the organization. They can be donors, suppliers, shareholder and other stakeholders. Without external communication, an organization would be isolated from its potential people.

The principles of effective communication are:

1- In addition to a sender there must also be a receiver or receivers, as the case may be, and both must be clearly identified.

2- There must be adequate method (or channel) of transmitting (passing) the communication, and should there be more than one channel available, the sender must select the most appropriate in the circumstances.

3- The sender must be sure that the language used in the communication is within the understanding of the intended receiver(s), and that the same interpretation will be put on the language at the receiving end as intended by the sender.

4- The sender must ensure that there is provision for feedback

5- The sender must be prepared to become a receiver as soon as there is a response (the feedback) to the communication.

6- Barriers or obstructions to or interferences with the smooth or clear flow of communications must be reduced or eliminated.

Feedback should be built into the communication network so that the senders of communications can check that they are being received, understood and acted upon. There are, unfortunately, some leaders on whose desks communication stop - information neither being passed upwards nor downwards, as the case may be. This lack of understanding on the part of those leaders gives rise to resentment and can cause many problems. It is important that all senior and junior leaders strictly avoid such damaging situations.

SUPERVISION

The work performed by teachers and any other workers must be supervised. Any instruction, guidance or training should be given when necessary. In addition, all operations or process must be checked / inspected, and performance must be measured against the set standards. For example the school can set the following standards: Finishing syllabus a month before examination; Repeating students should be 5% and below; Teachers should give a weekly test on all subjects.

An important part of the function of supervision entails the maintaining of records of performance. Such records are vital as guidance for future planning and setting up new standards. Supervision from higher offices in the schools should be encouraged to stimulate higher performance.

SCHOOL GOVERNING BODY (SGB)

In other countries like South Africa there is School Governing Bodies (SGB). The "governing body" is defined as the body that is entrusted with the responsibility and authority to formulate and adopt policy for each public school in terms of national policy and provincial education regulations. The governing body stands in a position of trust towards the school and fulfills the role of a public entity. The responsibility for financial management in some schools is delegated in the hands of the SGB of the school. Thus, the principal as a member of the SGB cannot make decision on his/her own. The school has to consult with all stakeholders on the SGB in relation to financial management of the school. The responsibilities of financial control entrusted to the SGB are probably their most important responsibilities; in particular, the preparation and approval of the annual budget. The SGB should perform the following mandatory financial functions:

- establish a school fund;
- collect and administer school fees;
- keep financial records;
- draw up annual financial statements; and
- Supplement state resources.

The role of principals and SGB has grown significantly over the years in most countries, among of which include increased diversity, greater leadership skills, strategic planning skills, budgeting and financial skills. It has also increased the power and responsibility of the principal, in terms of accountability to school community members. They also have the responsibility to work in collaborative way to achieve agreement. The principal is now very much viewed as an extension of the superintendent of the school at the school level.

Since financial management of schools is a relatively new concept in most schools, the burning question is whether principals and SGB have the essential training necessary to implement and effectively manage the finance. There is a clear distinction between governance, which is the responsibility of the SGB and professional management of schools, which means the day-to-day organization of teaching and learning, and the activities which support teaching and learning, for which teachers and principals are responsible.

SCHOOL PERFORMANCE APPRAISAL

Measuring school performance is imperative so that the school is able to outline areas that require attention from management. The appraisal reveals successes and challenges of the school in a particular year. The measurement also asserts gaps that are there in the school that makes it difficult to reach the desired goals.

After school performance appraisal, management can evaluate strategies that can help to uplift the performance of the school. If the used strategies did not work for the benefit of the school, management can replace them with new strategies.

School performance appraisal can be done in the following areas.

- Teachers' turnover

High teacher turnover implicates the performance of the school. The school faces a number of difficulties such as disturbed classes, confused students, stretched syllabus, students strike. The school should come up with measures to reduce teacher's turnover. Motivation of teachers is necessary to avoid high turnover. If the school has low teacher's turnover will indicate stability and continuity at the school which can help to improve the performance of the school.

- School resources

Insufficient of resources is another indicator for the school's poor performance. Underperforming school might have a direct correlation to insufficient of resources. If the school does not have enough books will make it difficult for the students and teachers in education system. The school can compare the previous year's number of the resources and the current year's and sees if there were positive changes.

- Students' pass rate

Students' pass rate is a tradition method many schools use to evaluate the success of the school. The higher pass rate of the school indicates higher performance of the school and lower pass rate of the school indicates the poor performance of the school and that may encourage a number of students to leave the school.

- Enrollment of students

The number of students enrolling at the school indicates the future of the school. If the school has a very limited number of students might close. The school needs to have a good enrollment every year. If enrollment decreases, management should evaluate reasons and bring strategies that can help to increase the number of students at the school.

- Number of students dropouts

Students' dropout decreases the number of students at school. If the number of dropouts increases at the school, management should find out the reasons and improves the situation to encourage good number of students.

- Increase of alumni

Former students can indicate the performance of the school. If there is a big number of former students that are successfully implementing knowledge gained at the school, inspires the currents students and put the school at higher position. A number of students will enroll at the school after understanding that many successful people studied at the school. The management needs to continue linking with graduating students to keep alumni department successful.

COMPARATIVE ANALYSIS

One of the tools that can be used to measure school performance is the comparative analysis. This is the tool whereby school performance is compared in four categories namely historical performance, competitor's performance, industry performance, best school performance.

Historical performance analysis: The school is able to measure its current performance to its previous performance. The school uses the historical data to measure the differences in the performance.

Competitor's performance analysis: The school compares its performance to the performance of the other schools in the district or region and sees if the school performed below them or above them. Relying on historical data might not give clear outlook of the performance of other schools. The school will be able to know reason why students leave to other schools or the reasons why students come to enroll at the school.

Industry performance analysis: This when the school compares its performance to the performance of the education department as a whole most probably by using the nation average schools performance. If the school performs below nation performance standard might be necessary for the management to improve the standard.

Best school performance analysis: This is when the school compares its performance to the best schools in the district, town, and country. Schools use this type of measurement when they want to put the school in the category of the best performers or when they want to take a leadership role.

IMPORTANCE OF EDUCATION

Education is a light that directs people to the right direction. For example, when a person is kept in a dark house and then ordered to look for gold and if he/she gets it must sell and use the money for his/her personal use will find it difficult as he/she might be using the assumptions to find the gold. The person can only come out with gold without hassles if he/she uses light. The light is education that people get to guide them to success. The uneducated people might find it difficult to make decisions.

Some governments restrict certain groups of people from acquiring education. The apartheid government of South Africa restricted the black people from getting good education. The apartheid government introduced Bantu education which was aimed for the black people. The Bantu education was perceived inferior compared to the white people education. The apartheid government wanted to fill unskilled labor economy with no white people. Those groups, which were given that opportunity to learn whatever they wanted, are much more advanced than those who were restricted. They possess good positions because they had good education. They are able to lead those who didn't have education.

Many uneducated people follow whatever the educated say, whether it is helping them or not. The apartheid government implemented the Bantu education policy to make white people leaders while non - white to become followers. In today's world most governments encourage citizens to take education seriously. Governments formulate policies that enable every citizen to get a chance of education.

The main problem that people are facing in many countries is not restriction of education but the lack of resources for the poor citizens. Many of them are not able to continue with their studies because they don't have funds. However they're many organizations and individuals who are dedicated to sponsor the poor citizens. Unfortunately some of the sponsoring organizations sponsor a student in the basis of color or race. If a person from another race group asks for sponsorship, restrictions are made or may be forced to choose courses that are cheap and not marketable.

A nation needs to produce good leaders, mathematicians, astronomers, physicians, doctors, judges, craftsmen, architects and many more skilled people. When people have no education they sometimes agree to things that may harm them and may fear things that may help them. Education gives confidence to a person. He is able to understand things faster than the uneducated.

Students should take education seriously so that they become important citizens of the country. However there should know that education does not come easily. It take perseverance and hardworking to reach the desired goal in education.

POEM- CROSSING BRIDGES OF THORNS

CROSSING BRIDGES OF THORNS

WALKING, RUNNING WITH HORSES OF HORNS

NIGHT AND DAY HOW TO CROSS OVER THE BRIDGES OF THORNS

BEAUTIFUL GARDENS AFTER THE BRIDGES OF THORNS

GARDEN OF COMFORT, TRANQUIL AND SMILE

BEAUTIFUL FLOWERS FROM BIG AND SMALL

ADVICE RUNS FROM ALL DIRECTIONS

HOW TO CROSS OVER THE BRIDGES OF THORNS

ADVICE FROM MUM AND DAD HOW TO CROSS

THE BRIDGES OF THORNS

EDUCATION IS FULL OF BRIDGES OF THORNS

YEARS AFTER YEARS TRYING TO CROSS OVER

THE BRIDGES OF THORNS

BACKED BY TANKERS, BOMBS TO CROSS OVER

THE BRIDGES OF THORNS

TANKERS, BOMBS FULL OF BOOKS, PENS TO CROSS OVER THE BRIDGES OF THORNS

TANKERS, BOMBS EMPOWERED BY SALARY OF

MUM AND DAD

SLEEPLESS MUM AND DAD HOW TO CROSS OVER BRIDGES OF THORNS

THERE IS BRIGHT FUTURE AFTER CROSSING

OVER THE BRIDGES OF THORNS

HELP ME DAD AND MUM TO CROSS OVER BRIDGES OF THORNS

HELP ME TEACHER TO CROSS OVER BRIDGES OF THORNS

TO GET COMFORT, TRANQUILITY AND SMILE

WITH HONOUR, DISCIPLINE, PATIENCE AND SACRIFICE

I CROSS OVER BRIDGES OF THORNS

EDUCATION IS FULL OF BRIDGES OF THORNS

By Manaf katonga

Conclusion

Education is the heart of a successful nation. A learning nation is a successful nation. The nation that fails to educate its citizens faces numerous challenges such as social problems, financial problems and political problems. But for the success of education to take place there should be good teachers to teach students. In many countries the number of good teachers is diminishing as the teaching career is becoming less attractive to a number of students because of the problems that are associated to teaching.

It is imperative for the governments to come up with measures to increase the number of teachers in schools. It is unchallenged that teachers are one of the vital elements of education. Therefore they need to be motivated and retained. Furthermore, education system can be effective if the students are disciplined and prepared to learn. It is very difficult for the teachers to impart knowledge to students that have barriers of education such as poor behavior. Therefore parents have an important role to play to ensure that students come to school prepared to learn and without any barrier of education.

It is the responsibility of the government and organizations to retain and motivate teachers. System of education will be successful if it is supported by the governments, organizations, communities, parents, learners and teachers. There should be good system in education to produce more teachers who will be responsible in educating the students. The death of a good system of education will make uneducated people leaders of the nations.